Irish Appropriation Of Greek Tragedy

Irish Appropriation Of Greek Tragedy

Brian Arkins

Caryfort Press

A Carysfort Press Book
Irish Appropriation Of Greek Tragedy
by
Brian Arkins
First published as a paperback in Ireland in 2009 by
Carysfort Press Ltd
58 Woodfield
Scholarstown Road
Dublin 16
 Ireland

ISBN 978-1-904505-47-1

Typeset by Carysfort Press Ltd

Printed and bound by eprint limited
Unit 35
Coolmine Industrial Estate
Dublin 15
Ireland
Cover design by eprint

This publication was grant-aided by the Publication Fund of the
National University of Ireland, Galway

This book is published with the financial assistance of
The Arts Council (An Chomhairle Ealaíon) Dublin, Ireland

For Anthony Roche

viro docto, amico caro

Contents

1 | A Brief Reading Of Greek Tragedy

1

Greek tragedy[1] should properly be termed 'Athenian tragedy' because Aeschylus, Sophocles, and Euripides were all Athenian citizens, and their plays were staged in the fifth century BC in the city (*polis*) of Athens. So to locate these tragedies in history, it is essential to analyse briefly what kind of place fifth century Athens was. In an apparent paradox, Athens was a city-state that was governed by a form of radical democracy, and that also ruled a considerable Empire.[2] Soon after Athens, in conjunction with other Greek states such as Sparta, defeated the forces of the Persian Empire in the period 490-79 BC, the city came to control the Aegean Sea with its numerous islands as an imperial power. The Athenian Empire embraced some 150 Greek communities, mainly in the Aegean, who paid annual tribute of money to Athens (a few states provided ships); the efficient silver mines at Laurion near Athens were also a major source of money. Some of this money went to finance artistic projects: while public money paid for the very expensive Parthenon, the private money of rich citizens paid for the staging of tragedies and comedies.

The acquisition of the Athenian Empire went hand in hand with a major political upheaval in Athens about the year 460 BC. The existing democracy that had been established by Cleisthenes in the late sixth century now became much more radical. All adult males who were citizens at birth were members of the Assembly (*Ekklesia*), and could attend its meetings; it is estimated that 6000 regularly did so. The Assembly exercised executive power over all political, financial, administrative, and legislative matters, as well as electing and dismissing magistrates such as the military *strategoi* and the civil *archontes*. The members of the Council of 500 (*Boute*), which prepared business for the Assembly, were elected by lot. Pay was introduced for magistrates, members of the Council, and jurymen serving in the law courts. This was a further radical move: 'Pay allowed all citizens, even the poorest, to perform time-consuming public tasks which they would otherwise not have had the leisure to fulfil, and thereby gave them a share in executive power'.3 That these political developments in Athens, the movement from aristocracy to democracy, paved the way for tragedy to flourish is suggested by the fact that, of the 31 extant tragedies, all but three were staged after 460 BC.4

Other Greek states, notably Sparta and Corinth, viewed Athenian imperialism with suspicion: Thucydides (1.23) explains that 'What made war inevitable was the growth of Athenian power and the fear which this caused in Sparta'5 (more specifically, Sparta's ally Corinth was uneasy at Athenian expansion). So Sparta went to war with Athens for much of the fifth century after 460 BC: the First Peloponnesian War lasted from 460 to 446 BC, and the Second Peloponnesian War lasted from 431 to 404 BC. The Second Peloponnesian War was a disaster for Athens: it lost the war to Sparta, and its control of the Aegean ended after three quarters of a century, with widespread revolts ensuing; Athens was never to regain the same prominence in Greek affairs. The sheer length of the Peloponnesian War ensured that many of the extant tragedies were composed during it, and that a significant number of them – such as Euripides' *The Trojan Women* (415 BC) – deal with the theme of war.

2

The circumstances in which Athenian tragedies were performed were different in virtually every respect from those of contemporary theatre.6 In the modern world, tragedies, like every other form of play, are staged either in the commercial theatre, or in art-house venues, or in amateur productions, and are put on for a run during which they are performed each night (or at matinées). But in fifth century Athens, tragedies were staged only during brief festivals of the god Dionysus, and will have taken place from early morning until about midday. The festivals in Athens were the Great Dionysia in March-April (the time when the god died and rose again), and the Lenaia (feast of the wine-vats) in January-February; the rural Dionysia took place in December in the 140 or so localities in Attica. The tragedies in Athens were staged in the theatre of Dionysus or the southern slopes of the Acropolis, which was a tiered semi-circular construction with excellent acoustics.

Tragedies were therefore part of a religious festival that also had distinct political aspects:[7] the ten generals (*strategoi*) made libations to Dionysus; the tribute of Athenian allies was brought into the theatre; the names of the benefactors of Athens were read out; and the children of those who died in war were paraded in full military uniform. A further aspect of state involvement in Athenian tragedy is that the three playwrights who wrote tragedies for the Great Dionysia were chosen in mid-summer of the previous year by a magistrate, the Eponymous Archon (a role performed for the Lenaia by the King Archon); again, the elaborate costumes of the chorus were paid for by rich citizens. When a playwright was chosen by the Archon, he had to write four plays, three tragedies which might or might not be connected in theme, and a satyr-play, which had a Chorus consisting of satyrs, the wild attendants of Dionysus, and which explores 'human culture through a fun-house mirror'.[8] The three playwrights were in competition with each other, as befitted a society that was intensely agonistic, and there were first, second, and third prizes. Aeschylus won thirteen first prizes, Sophocles twenty-four, and Euripides four. The production of a fifth century tragedy was a unique event, and it was not until 387 BC that an old play was restaged.

The number of actors in Athenian tragedy was much more circumscribed than in the modern theatre. Aeschylus introduced a second actor and Sophocles a third, that being the maximum allowed. All the actors, who were citizens, were male, so that female parts were played by men. The leading actor (who was paid and competed for a prize) needed to be a skilled solo singer, and will have played a major part in plays: so in Sophocles' *King Oedipus*, the first actor played Oedipus, and the other two played seven parts between them. Actors wore masks (Dionysus was the god of the mask), which meant that changes of facial expression were impossible and that the voice became paramount; Yeats held that Greek acting 'did all but everything with the voice'.[9] Actors also wore a head-dress, a long robe, and boots (*kothornoi*), so that they appeared to be remote impressive figures, an example of Brecht's 'alienation effect'.

The Chorus, which consisted of twelve (later fifteen members), was an essential part of fifth century tragedy. The fact that they danced and sang ensured that they were both linked to cultic practice, and were able to provide great entertainment. While the Chorus may not always have revealed their position, their major function was to provide a collective response to what happened in the play, but they express very often 'the experience of the excluded, the oppressed, and the vulnerable'.[10] Yeats held that the Chorus alleviated the monotony of a Greek play's concentration on a single idea, served to check the rapidity of the dialogue, and provided the emotion of multitude by calling up famous sorrows.[11] Indeed Yeats uses a type of Chorus in *The Shadowy Waters* (sailors) and in *Deirdre* (musicians). As time went on, the importance of the Chorus lessened: in Aeschylus, the Chorus takes up about half the play, in Euripides about a quarter.

There was a large attendance at tragedies in fifth century Athens, probably about 15,000, and poor people may have been given a grant to attend from the Theoric fund; the amount of money involved was small, but was a powerful symbol of Athenian commitment to democracy. The bulk of the attendance consisted of adult male citizens, but foreigners and resident aliens (metics) also attended. Whether women attended is a hotly contested issue; the answer is that we do not know.[12] Certain men had special seats at the theatre: the priest of Dionysus, magistrates, members of the Council (*Boule*). This disparate audience in Athens contrasts with that of the modern theatre: 'In the main, it consists of persons who are extraordinarily well educated, whose incomes are very high, who are predominantly in the professions, and who are in their late youth or early middle age'.[13]

All in all, the tragedies of fifth century Athens were an integral part of the life of the community, the notion of 'art for art's sake' not being found before the Hellenistic period (321-31 BC). But it is striking that, while those tragedies may affirm the *status quo* in their society, they also consistently *problematize* important issues like war, feminism, and religion; as Croally says, 'tragedy questions ideology'.[14] Hence the Athenians deconstructed their own society before anyone else did. Which may help to explain the perennial popularity of Aeschylus, Sophocles, and Euripides, copies of whose plays were placed in the state depositary at Athens in the 330s BC.

3

Another way in which Athenian tragedy of the fifth century BC differed to a significant degree from modern theatre is in its subject-matter, myth. In structuralist terms, mythology functions as a system of signs that imposes order on human experience and especially on conflict; in symbolist theory, myth represents structures considered to be universal, to be archetypes. Either way, these stories of Greek mythology – called by Wallace Stevens 'the greatest piece of fiction'15 – remain perennially fascinating.

There were cogent reasons, negative and positive, for Athenian tragedians to make use of myth. A negative argument in favour of myth was that contemporary subjects could be dangerous. After the city of Miletus in Asia Minor, which had close ties with Athens, was destroyed by the Persians in 494 BC, the Athenian playwright Phrynichus wrote a tragedy called *The Fall of Miletus*. This was too close to the bone for the audience, who were very distressed by the city's destruction, and burst into tears, with the result that Phrynichus was fined 1,000 drachmas (Herodotus 6.21). It is also worth noting that, although Athenian comedy regularly dealt with contemporary matters, Aristophanes was apparently prosecuted in 426 BC because his play *Babylonians* attacked local politicians. (The only extant tragedy dealing with contemporary events is *The Persians* of Aeschylus.)

Myth enjoyed two very important advantages over contemporary material: it made use of a distancing technique, and it was inherently flexible. Because the stories of myth are set in a distant, remote past they can be enlisted to comment in an oblique way on what is going on in the present, without appearing to do so. So Euripides' tragedy *The Trojan Women* appears to deal with the Trojan war, but, since it was put on in Athens in 415 BC during the Peloponesian War, it clearly comments on that event. Similarly, in the modern world many playwrights who appropriate Greek myth do so with the intent of commenting on contemporary events – as Tom Paulin's *The Riot Act*, based on *Antigone*, deals with Northern Ireland.

An equally important advantage of Greek myth is its flexibility: since there is no such thing as a definitive version of any Greek story, the dramatist is free to innovate, provided he maintains the invariant core: Oedipus must kill his father, marry his mother. In Euripides' *Medea*, it is almost certain that the Athenian dramatist invented the murder of her children by Medea, thus adding greatly to the pathos and horror of the story. Greek tragedy often involves one author using the conflicts of myths in an individual way.

Extant Greek tragedy focuses almost entirely on four cycles of myth: 16 plays deal with the Trojan cycle, 6 plays with the Theban cycle, 4 plays with Herakles, and 4 plays with the legendary history of Athens; that is, 30 out of 31 plays. As Aristotle says (*Poetics* 1454), 'tragedies are concerned with a few families'. While this may seem a very narrow canvas, in practice it has given us a large number of plays that are central to the European theatrical corpus.

4

In seeking to isolate the main characteristics of Athenian tragedy, we inevitably begin with the account of Aristotle in the *Poetics*, a work written between 367 and 322 BC that is less a treatise on aesthetics than a handbook on how to write a tragedy.[16] For Aristotle, the *action* of the tragedy is paramount, and character is secondary; what happens is what counts. Aristotle holds that tragedy provides an 'imitation' (*mimesis*) of that action, or what is now termed 'representation'; as Brecht says, tragedy offers 'live representations of reported or invented happenings between human beings'.[17] Often the action of the tragedy involves horrific incidents – Aristotle's 'scene of suffering' – such as the suicide of Jocasta or the self-blinding of Oedipus in Sophocles' *King Oedipus*.

Such incidents arise out of *hamartia* on the part of the protagonist, a word that denotes 'a mistake', an error; it cannot be too strongly stressed that *hamartia* does not mean 'a fatal flaw', a concept that has no place in Athenian tragedy.[18] So in *King Oedipus*, Oedipus makes the mistake of marrying a woman old enough to be his mother (who was his mother), and of killing a man old enough to be his father (who was his father). (In Shakespearean tragedy, the tragic flaw is found by some critics: the ambition of Macbeth, the inaction of Hamlet, the jealousy of Othello; Father Butt (in reality Fr. Darlington) in Joyce's *Stephen Hero* sees the moral of Othello as 'an object lesson in the passion of jealousy'.[19])

As the mistake(s) of the protagonist lead to horrific events, he may experience a realization of what his position actually is (*anagnorisis*), such knowledge underlining the highly cognitive nature of Athenian tragedy. That knowledge may also lead to an astonishing reversal of fortune for the tragic hero (*peripeteia*), which Aristotle holds should be from good fortune to bad. Hence in *King Oedipus*, when Oedipus realizes that he is the son of Laius and Jocasta, that he has committed parricide and incest, he changes from being a powerful king to being a blind nonentity.

In an early example of reception theory, Aristotle stated that the horrific incidents in Athenian tragedy arouse pity and fear in the spectator, and lead to the catharsis of these emotions. The spectator pities the suicide of Jocasta because she is subjectively innocent, and fears that he might be subjected to such a fate in the future. So for Aristotle, art is kinetic, as it was not for Stephen Dedalus in Joyce's *Portrait*: though art, 'The mind is arrested and raised above desire and loathing'.[20] The meaning of catharsis when applied to tragedy is one of the most disputed issues in classical scholarship: it may denote 'purgation', or 'purification', or 'intellectual clarification'. The meaning of 'purification' suggests the dross is removed from pity and fear. The meaning of 'purgation' suggests that aesthetic experience triumphs over emotions. But 'intellectual clarification'[21] has the great merit of fitting in with the stress on knowledge in Athenian tragedy.

Whatever the meaning of catharsis, it is clear that it involves for the spectator a form of pleasure; as Brecht says, catharsis 'is a purification which is performed not only in a pleasurable way, but precisely for the purpose of pleasure'.[22] The nature of this pleasure that the spectator takes in tragedy seems closely linked to *Schadenfreude*: he is pleased that horrific things are happening to someone else, and not to him; as Burke said, 'I am convinced we have a degree of delight, and that no small one, in the real misfortunes and pains of others'.[23] (Related to this is the fact that the spectator can readily bear in art what would be intolerable in real life.) A further Nietzschean form of *Schadenfreude* is taking pleasure in the type of cosmic ruin that often ends tragedies, what Yeats memorably terms 'God's laughter at the shattering of the world';[24] here elements of sadism and the death-wish coalesce.

5

One further concept that Aristotle stresses – suffering – brings us close to the essence of tragedy, with Schopenhauer maintaining that 'the presentation of a great misfortune is alone essential' to tragedy.[25] The essence of tragedy therefore chimes with the fact that suffering is pervasive in human life; as Adorno said, 'The One and All that keeps rolling on to this day – with occasional breathing spells – would teleologically be the absolute of suffering'.[26] Or as Hopkins puts it, when addressing a young child called Margaret, who is upset at the falling of leaves in the autumn: 'It is the blight man was born for,/It is Margaret you mourn for'.[27]

In Athenian tragedy, such suffering often arises out of a conflict (*agon*) between two characters. So the conflict between Antigone and Creon leads to her death and his ruin; the conflict between Medea and Jason leads to her murder of their children and his ruin; the conflict between Peonthus and Dionysus leads to the killing and dismemberment of the king by the Bacchantes. The horror of these events, the great suffering involved, is not lessened by the fact that they are not (usually) portrayed on stage, but related by a Messenger.

The question that then arises is: why this suffering? Since the best efforts of philosophers and theologians have failed to provide any definitive answer to this question[28] it is unreasonable to expect tragic dramatists to answer it. The kind of cognition provided by tragedy is not at all that of metaphysical certainty, but much more akin to Keats' concept of 'negative capability': 'when man is capable of being in uncertainties, Mysteries, doubts, without any irritable reaching after fact and reason'.[29] Hence Leech rightly sees tragedy telling us 'what we have to face, and we do not know, and we cannot quarrel with the dramatist for not letting us, how to face it'.[30]

The great suffering experienced by characters in tragedy can be partially alleviated by heroic acceptance of what has happened, so that 'man is splendid in his ashes'.[31] For Yeats, Macbeth, Anthony, and Hamlet face their fate with tragic joy:

> The heroes of Shakespeare convey to us through their looks, or through the metaphorical patterns of their speech, the sudden enlargement of their vision, their ecstasy at the approach of death: 'She should have died hereafter', 'Of many thousand kisses, the poor last', 'Absent thee from felicity awhile'.[32]

So too Oedipus in his two name-plays exhibits a noble acceptance of his fate.

The fact that Athenian tragedy is pervaded by suffering and that many of the plays end with one or more deaths does not mean that their *Weltanschauung* is uniformly bleak: a significant number of these tragedies end on a positive note, have a 'happy ending'. So in Aeschylus' trilogy *Oresteia*, the apparently endless cycle of tit-for-tat killings is brought to an end by the Court of the Areopagus in Athens. So in Sophocles' *Philoctetes*, the *deus ex machina* of Herakles ensures that Philoctetes and the Greeks are reconciled. So a significant number of Euripides' tragedies have a positive ending: these include *Alcestis* where the protagonist is rescued from Death; *Orestes* where the protagonist will be freed and will marry Hermione; *Helen* where Helen and Menelaus escape on a ship; and *Ion* where the abandoned Ion is recognized as the child of Creusa, and becomes the ancestor of the Ionian race. Some of these plays, and notably Ion, blur the distinction between tragedy and comedy; indeed subsequent recognition of an exposed child and the happy consequences are typical of Greek New Comedy as practised by Menander (342-c.292 BC) and others.

That Athenian tragedy is not always dark is pointed up by the tragedies of Seneca[33] (c.4 BC-65 AD) that present an overwhelming stress on the triumph of evil, which is centred in the ruler and against which reason is unavailing. In Seneca, there is no hint whatsoever that the cosmos can be benign; *au contraire*, it is always utterly malign. Though these tragedies are based on Greek myth, they clearly relate to the iniquities of Nero in contemporary Rome and Seneca's failure as an advisor to control them; they therefore provide a major example of how Greek myth can be used to comment on the contemporary world. And the artistic value of Seneca's tragedies can be seen in the fact that his stress on evil in the ruler was appropriated by Shakespeare, most notably in *Titus Andronicus*, but also in *Macbeth* and in *Richard III*.[34]

6

One feature of Athenian tragedies that requires special comment is the very significant role played in them by women.[35] (Only one extant play, *Philoctetes*, has no women characters, while female choruses outnumber male ones by 21 to 10.)

In Athens, aristocratic women were virtually confined to the house (*oikos*), and had no role to play in the city (*polis*) – apart from participating in a number of religious festivals. Women, who entered an arranged marriage at about the age of fourteen, were defined by the social significance of their bodies, by their ability to produce children and especially boys who would continue the citizen line. As the sentence uttered by the bride's father to the groom at the engagement ceremony graphically indicates: 'I give you this women for the ploughing of legitimate children.' In so far as romantic love existed in Athens, it took the form of a sexual relationship between an older man, who was or would be married, and an adolescent boy between the ages of twelve and eighteen.

Put the other way round, Athenian men controlled everything of importance in the city: politics, the army, the navy, the lawcourts, commerce, agriculture, the Olympic and other Games. In reality, therefore, Athenian aristocratic women led extremely restricted lives; in Greek literature, on the other hand, and particularly in tragedy and comedy, women play a very prominent role. This paradox struck Virginia Woolf forcefully in 1929:

> If women had no existence save in the fiction written by men, one would imagine her a person of the utmost importance; very various; heroic and mean; splendid and sordid; infinitely beautiful and hideous in the extreme; as great as a man, some think even greater. But this woman is in fiction. In fact ... she was locked up, beaten and flung about the rooms. A very queer, composite being thus emerges. Imaginatively she is of the highest importance; practically she is completely insignificant. She pervades poetry from cover to cover; she is all but absent from history. She dominates the lives of kings and conquerors in fiction; in fact she was the slave of any boy whose parents fixed a ring upon her finger. Some of the most inspired words, some of the most profound thoughts in literature fall from her lips; in real life she could hardly read, could scarcely spell, and was the property of her husband.[36]

The classicist Helene Foley has remarked on the same paradox in regard to Athenian women:

> Although women in fact play virtually no public role other than a religious one in the political and social life of ancient Greece, they dominate the imaginative life of Greek men to a degree almost unparalleled in the Western tradition ... Greek writers used the female – in a fashion that bore little relation to the lives of actual women – to understand, express, criticize, and experiment with the problems and contradictions of their culture.[37]

What happens, then, in Athenian tragedy is that male playwrights use their *imagination* to create powerful female roles, so that art triumphs over life. At the same time, these powerful women can be related to Athenian reality: they often act in the absence of their husband or guardian (*kurios*) in a way that disrupts the male system, and this pattern 'can be interpreted as a symptom of the Athenian citizen's anxiety about the crises which might affect his household during his absence'.[38]

7

The suffering that pervades Athenian tragedy and the pleasure derived from it are presented by its authors with exquisite art; as Beckett says, 'To find a form that accommodates the mess, that is the task of the artist'.[39] In *The Birth of Tragedy* (1872),[40] Nietzsche uses the gods Dionysus and Apollo in a symbolic way, so that the suffering of the individual person is associated with Dionysus and the clarity of tragic art with Apollo. For Nietzsche, Dionysus' role as the god of fertility, of wild nature, of wine, of ritual sacrifice and ecstatic worship, of mythic dismemberment, symbolizes the dark irrational side of the Greeks that can cause horror. On the other hand, Apollo's role as leader and as god of music and poetry symbolizes light, clarity, restraint, beauty and form that can give aesthetic pleasure. Hence for Nietzsche, Athenian plays constitute a 'work of art that is as Dionysiac as it is Apolline – Attic tragedy'.[41] That the Greek gods were present in Athenian tragedy is attested by Yeats in relation to King Oedipus:

> In rehearsal I had but one overwhelming emotion, a sense of the actual presence in a terrible sacrament of the god. But I have got that always, though never before so strongly, from Greek drama.[42]

In formal terms,[43] Athenian tragedy alternates between scenes and choral odes. Written in the iambic metre that Aristotle saw as closest to human speech (compare Shakespeare's iambic pentameter), and in Attic Greek, the scenes are divided into speeches of varying length made by characters and stichomythia, in which two or more characters exchange (usually) one line statements. Written in a wide variety of metres and in partly Doric dialect, the choral odes are sung by a group to the accompaniment of music and dancing.[44]

While the Athenian tragedians manipulate the archaic, but highly prestigious diction of the Greek bible, Homer, their language is, as Goldhill says, 'public, democratic male talk'.[45] So the language of law in the shape of a courtroom scene is found in Aeschylus' play *Eumenides*, while that of religious ritual is found in the account of Pentheus' death in Euripides' play *The Bacchae*. So too the tragedians, and especially Euripides, drew on the techniques of rhetoric used by the group of teachers called the Sophists to debate contemporary issues. Such debate can exemplify the fact that language is not a fixed entity where words precisely denote something, but is, rather, liable to subjective interpretation. For example, in Aeschylus' play *The Suppliant Women*, the noun *kratos* – which has meanings such as 'rule', 'power', 'force' – is used by King Pelasgus to refer to 'legitimate authority', but by the suppliant women to mean 'violent force'.[46]

A striking feature of the art of Athenian tragedies is their brevity and resulting concentration (*King Oedipus* has 1530 lines); as Yeats said, 'A Greek play, unlike a Shakespearian play, is the exposition of one idea'.[47] Such concentrated brevity ensures that the Athenian plays often exhibit the sense of inevitability attributed to tragedy by Anouilh in his *Antigone*:[48]

> The spring is wound up tight. It will uncoil of itself. That is what is so convenient in tragedy. The least little turn of the wrist will do the job ... The rest is automatic. You don't need to lift a finger. The machine is in perfect order; it has been oiled ever since time began, and it runs without friction. Death, treason and sorrow are on the march ...

8

To conclude. Tragedy has often been seen as a uniquely valuable form of art; for Richards, 'Tragedy is perhaps the most general, all-accepting, all-ordering experience known'.[49] But others have maintained that comedy is to be preferred because it includes more aspects of human life within it; Kavanagh held that 'Tragedy is underdeveloped Comedy'.[50] One way of formulating the difference between the two genres is to say that tragedy belongs to the soul or spirit, comedy to the body. Certainly, nobody in Athenian tragedy eats or drinks, urinates or defecates; and while sex is a pervasive theme there, it is always handled in a highly elevated way that contrasts with the ribaldry and obscenity of Aristophanic comedy.

Ultimately, the question of whether tragedy or comedy is the superior form may be unanswerable. When Beckett (who termed *Waiting for Godot* a 'tragi-comedy') was asked by Desmond Egan to adjudicate between comedy and tragedy, he declined to come down on one side or the other:[51]

> Sorry I can't help with yr. problem.
> Democritus laughed at Heraclitus
> weeping + H. wept at D. laughing.
> Pick yr. fancy.

Consequently, the same man, said Socrates at the end of Plato's *Symposium*, should be able to write both tragedy and comedy. A Russian exemplar of this is Chekhov and an Irish exemplar Synge: *Riders to the Sea* has all the inevitability of an Athenian tragedy (for Yeats, it is Aeschylus and Sophocles combined);[52] *The Playboy of the Western World* is a comedy that inverts the parricide theme of *King Oedipus*.

---

[1] For tragedy in general see, e.g., F. Ferguson, *The Idea of a Theatre* (Princeton: Princeton University Press, 1949); C. Leech, *Tragedy* (London: Methuen, 1969); T.R. Henn, *The Harvest of Tragedy* (London: Methuen, 1966); *Tragedy*, eds. J. Drakakis and N.C. Liebler

(London: Longman, 1998); T. Eagleton, *Sweet Violence – The Idea of the Tragic* (Oxford: Blackwell, 2003); A. Poole, *Tragedy* (Oxford: Oxford University Press, 2005). For Greek tragedy see, e.g., H.D.F. Kitto, *Form and Meaning in Drama* (London: Methuen, 1956); A. Lesky, *Greek Tragedy* (London: Ernest Benn 1967); J.-P. Vernant and P. Vidal-Naquet, *Myth and Tragedy in Ancient Greece* (Cambridge, Mass.: Zone Books, 1988); *Tragedy and the Tragic*, ed. M.S. Silk (Oxford: Oxford University Press 1996); *The Cambridge Companion to Greek Tragedy*, ed. P.E. Easterling (Cambridge: Cambridge University Press 1997); P. Wilson in *Literature in the Greek World*, ed. O. Taplin (Oxford: Oxford University Press, 2001), pp. 70-114; N. Loraux, *The Mourning Voice – An Essay on Greek Tragedy* (Ithaca/London: Cornell University Press, 2002).

[2] For Athenian democracy and the Athenian Empire see R. Meiggs, *The Athenian Empire* (Oxford: Oxford University Press, 1972); M.I. Finley, *Economy and Society in Ancient Greece* (Harmondsworth: Penguin, 1983), pp. 41-61; J.K. Davies, *Democracy and Classical Greece* (London: Fontana, 1978); S. Hornblower, *The Greek World 479-323 BC* (London: Routledge, 2002).

[3] Davies (note 2), p. 69.

[4] The three are by Aeschylus: *The Persians* (472 BC), *The Seven Against Thebes* (467 B.C.), and the *Suppliant Women* (probably 463 BC). The figure of 31 extant tragedies involves regarding Aeschylus' *Prometheus Bound* and Euripides' *Rhesus* as spurious.

[5] Translation by Rex Warner.

[6] A.W. Pickard-Cambridge, *The Dramatic Festivals of Athens* (Oxford: Oxford University Press, 1988).

[7] S. Goldhill in *The Cambridge Companion* (note 1), p. 56.

[8] F. Lissarrague in J.J. Winkler and F. Zeitlin eds., *Nothing to do with Dionysus: Athenian Drama in its Social Context* (Princeton: Princeton University Press, 1990), pp. 233-36.

[9] W.B. Yeats, *Explorations* (London: Macmillan, 1962), p.110. For Greek Themes in Yeats see B. Arkins, *Builders of My Soul: Greek and Roman Themes in Yeats* (Gerrards Cross: Colin Smythe, 1990).

[10] J. Gould in Silk (note 1), p. 224.

[11] W.B. Yeats, quoted in K. Dorn, *Players and Painted Stage – The Theatre of W.B. Yeats* (Brighton: Harvester Press, 1984), pp. 76-77; W.B. Yeats, *Essays and Introductions* (London: Macmillan, 1961), p. 233; p. 215.

[12] Goldhill (note 5), pp. 62-66. For theatre audiences see S. Bennett, *Theatre Audiences* (London: Routledge, 2003).

[13] Baumol and Boun, quoted in Bennett (note 11), p. 87.

[14] N.T. Croally, *Euripidean Polemic* (Cambridge: Cambridge University Press, 1994), p. 43.

[15] Wallace Stevens, *Opus Posthumous*, ed. S.F. Morse, London, 1959, p. 178.

[16] For the *Poetics* see, e.g., G.F. Else, *Aristotle's Poetics* (Harvard: Harvard University Press, 1957); L. Golden and O.B. Hardison, Jr., *Aristotle's Poetics* (Englewood Cliffs, N.J.: Prentice-Hall, 1968); S. Halliwell, *The*

Poetics of Aristotle, London, 1987; M. Heath, *Aristotle – Poetics*, (London: Penguin, 1996).

[17] Brecht, quoted in Drakakis and Liebler (note 1), p. 88.

[18] J.-M. Bremer, *Hamartia: Tragic Error in the Poetics of Aristotle and in Greek Tragedy* (Amsterdam: Rodopi, 1969).

[19] James Joyce, *Stephen Hero* (London: Granada, 1981), p. 32. For rejection of 'the fatal flaw' in Shakespeare see F. O'Toole, *Shakespeare is Hard but so is Life* (London/New York: Granta Books, 2002).

[20] James Joyce, *A Portrait of the Artist as a Young Man* (Harmondsworth: Penguin, 1960), p. 205.

[21] Golden (note 16), pp. 116-18.

[22] Brecht, quoted in Drakakis and Liebler (note 1), 89. For the pleasure of tragedy see Henn (note 1), pp. 43-58; A.D. Nuttall, *Why Does Tragedy Give Pleasure?* (Oxford: Oxford University Press, 1996); Eagleton (note 1), pp. 153-77.

[23] Burke, quoted in Henn (note 1), p. 54.

[24] W.B. Yeats, *Collected Plays* (London: Macmillan, 1960), p. 114.

[25] A. Schopenhauer, *The World as Will and Representation* (New York, 1969), p. 1, p. 254.

[26] T.W. Adorno, *Negative Dialectics* (London: Longman, 1973), p. 320.

[27] *The Poems of Gerard Manley Hopkins*, eds. W.H. Gardner and H.N. MacKenzie (Oxford: Oxford University Press, 1970), p. 89.

[28] Cf. T.W. Tilley, 'Evil Problem of' in *The New Dictionary of Theology*, eds. J.A. Komanchek, M. Collins, and D.A. Lane (Dublin: Gill & Macmillan, 1987), pp. 360-63; : M.A. Fatula, OP, 'Suffering', *ibid.*, pp. 990-92.

[29] *Letters of John Keats*, ed. F. Page (London: Longman, 1954), p.53.

[30] Leech (note 1), p. 50.

[31] Henn (note 1), p. 288.

[32] Yeats, 1961 (note 11), p. 288.

[33] For Senecan tragedy, see, e.g., C.J. Herington, *Arion* 5(1966), pp. 422-71; D. Henry and B. Walker, *The Mask of Power: Seneca's Tragedies and Imperial Rome* (Warminster: Aris & Phillips, 1985); A.J. Boyle, *Ramus* 18(1989), pp. 78-101; *id.*, *Tragic Seneca: An essay in the Theatrical Tradition* (London: Routledge, 1997).

[34] For Seneca's impact on Shakespeare see B. Arkins, *Classics Ireland* 2(1995), pp. 1-16.

[35] For women in tragedy see E. Hall in *The Cambridge Companion* (note 1), pp. 103-10; S.B. Pomeroy, *Goddesses, Whores, Wives, and Slaves* (London: Pimlico, 1994), pp. 93-112.

[36] Virginia Woolf, *A Room of One's Own* (London: Hogarth Press, 1929), pp. 45-46.

[37] H. Foley in *Civilization of the Ancient Mediterranean: Greece and Rome*, ed. M. Grant and R. Kitzinger (New York, 1988), pp. 130-32.

[38] Hall (note 35), p. 107.

[39] Beckett, quoted in *The Cambridge Companion to Beckett*, ed. Pillins (Cambridge: Cambridge University Press, 1996), p. 74.

40 For *The Birth of Tragedy* see M.S. Silk and J.P. Stern, *Nietzsche on Tragedy* (Cambridge: Cambridge University Press, 1981); M. Tanner, *Nietzsche* (Oxford: Oxford University Press, 1996), pp. 7-18. For Nietzsche and the Classics see H. Lloyd-Jones, *Blood for the Ghosts* (London: Duckworth, 1982), pp. 165-81.

41 Nietzsche, *The Birth of Tragedy*.

42 *The Letters of W.B. Yeats*, ed. A. Wade (London: Rupert Hart-Davis, 1950), p. 720.

43 S. Goldhill in *The Cambridge Companion* (note 1), pp. 127-50.

44 M. West, *Ancient Greek Music* (Oxford: Oxford University Press, 1992); A. Henrichs, 'Why should I dance?', *Arion* 3(1995), pp. 56-111.

45 Goldhill (note 43), p. 128.

46 J.-P. Vernant and P. Vidal Naquet, *Myth and Tragedy in Ancient Greece* (Cambridge, Mass.: Zone Books, 1988), p. 39.

47 W.B. Yeats, quoted by K. Dorn, *Players and Painted Stage – The Theatre of W.B. Yeats* (Brighton: Harvester Press, 1984), p. 77.

48 Jean Anouilh, *Antigone*, Paris, 1984, p. 66; English translation by L. Galantière, quoted in Leech (note 1), p. 8.

49 I.A. Richards, *Principles of Literary Criticism* (London: Routledge & Kegan Paul, 1967), p. 194.

50 Patrick Kavanagh, *Collected Poems* (London: Martin Brian & O'Keeffe, 1973), p. xiv.

51 Beckett, quoted by V. Abbott in *Desmond Egan – The Poet and his Work*, ed. H. Kenner (Orono: Northern Lights, 1990), p. 52.

52 For Yeats's verdict see R. Best in *J.M. Synge – Interviews and Recollections*, ed. E.N. Mikhail (London: Longman, 1977), p. 120.

2 | Irish Appropriation of Greek Tragedy: An Overview

1

The achievement of Athenian tragedy in the fifth century BC has often, in later eras, seemed to be unsurpassable, and has lent itself to hyperbole. Milton held that Aeschylus, Sophocles, and Euripides are 'unequalled, yet by any, and the best rule to all who endeavour to write tragedy'. In similar vein, Ricoeur finds that, since the plays encapsulate the essence of tragedy, 'we can understand all other tragedy as analogous to Greek tragedy'. For Virginia Woolf, it is the women and men in Athenian tragedy who function as paradigm: in the plays, 'the stable, the permanent, the original human being is to be found'. The classic Irish statement of this type was made by Yeats at the very end of his life in 1939:

> The Greek drama alone achieved perfection; it has never been done since; it may be thousands of years before we achieve that perfection again. Shakespeare is only a mass of magnificent fragments'.[1]

To which hyperbole Dr. Leavis might reply that we cannot read Shakespeare as we read Aeschylus.[2]

Not every era could appreciate the brilliance of Athenian tragedy, for in the Middle Ages there was no clear grasp of what a tragedy is. Hence in Borges' short story 'Averroes' Search',[3] the mediaeval Islamic philosopher Averroes (1126-98) can write 38 commentaries on Aristotle, but is unable to hazard a guess as to the meaning of 'tragedy' and of 'comedy'; eventually, he defines them as 'panegyric' and 'satire' respectively. In the modern era, the problem is different: while we know what tragedy is, it is not clear to everyone that it can still be written. So critics like George Steiner believe that tragedy cannot be produced in the modern secular, democratic world, but Weitz counters this with the assertion that 'It is simply a historical fact that the concept, as we know it and use it, has continuously accommodated new cases of tragedy and, more important, the new properties of these cases'.[4]

Already in the Greco-Roman world, there was a feeling that tragedy did not always proceed on a consistently elevated course: in Aristophanes' comedy *The Frogs*, the character Euripides claims that he has made tragedy 'democratic' (*démokratikon*) by having women and slaves talk alongside their master; Horace notes that, when tragic characters like Telephus or Peleus are in dire straits, they use ordinary, non-tragic language.[5] In the eighteenth century, Lessing advocated, instead of the portrayal of kings and queens, what he called 'bürgerliches Trauerspiel', 'a tragedy of citizens', and produced an example in his play *Nathan the Wise*, whose hero is a bourgeois. Lessing's view adumbrates the way in which tragedies in the modern world can concern themselves with women and with men who are not of exalted rank. Hence the theatre of Ibsen, Strindberg, and Chekhov deals with the fate of the bourgeois, while that of Miller, Williams, and O'Neill deals with the fate of the proletariat. And the predominant literary form of the modern world, the novel, can also be tragic: as in Dostoevsky, Conrad, and, above all, Kafka.[6] A point eloquently made by Balzac in his novel *Eugénie Grandet*: this novel is 'a bourgeois tragedy undignified by poison, dagger, or bloodshed, but to the protagonists more cruel than any of the tragedies endured by members of the noble house of Atreus'.[7]

2

Tragedy can be written in the modern world, but in the late nineteenth and early twentieth centuries, tragedies were written not in the major centres of European capitalism, but in peripheral regions such as Scandinavia, Russia, and Ireland;[8] hence Yeats and Synge wrote tragedies during the Irish Literary Renaissance in the first decade of the twentieth century.[9] (Yeats continued to write tragedies until his death in 1939.)

The circumstances in which Yeats and Synge were writing plays in the early years of the twentieth century were very favourable to the production of tragedy. For it was the aim of the Literary Renaissance and of the Abbey theatre in Dublin to dignify Ireland by staging tragic drama that would exploit both contemporary settings and ancient Celtic myth. Hence the tragic death of Deirdre, the Irish

Helen in both Yeats's *Deirdre* and Synge's *Deirdre of the Sorrows*, the death of Cuchulain, the Irish Achilles, in Yeats's *On Baile's Strand*, and the multiple deaths of fishermen in Synge's *Riders to the Sea*. As Leech says, 'we can see Dublin as the one place in the earliest years of this century where tragedy in the English language was boldly and simply essayed and firmly achieved'.[10]

Later, in the 1920s, O'Casey uses the term 'tragedy' to describe three plays that depict women and men who live in Dublin tenements: *The Shadow of the Gunman* (1923), *Juno and the Paycock* (1924), and *The Plough and the Stars* (1926). The tension that existed in fifth century Athens between the civic ideology associated with tragedy and the content of the plays performed was replicated in Ireland in 1926 when O'Casey's *The Plough and the Stars* was staged at the Abbey.[11] Because the play represented the rebels of the Easter Rising as cowardly and vain, it was attacked by republican women. Because the play portrayed a prostitute on stage, the Government, which had recently made the Abbey a subsidized theatre, objected.

During the period of the Irish Free State (1922-1948) and of the Republic of Ireland (1948-), Irish playwrights have continued to write tragedies.[12] A representative (though obviously partial) list would include: Teresa Deevey, *Katie Roche* (1936); Samuel Beckett, *Endgame* (1957); Tom Murphy, *A Whistle in the Dark* (1960); J.B. Keane, *The Field* (1965); Tom Kilroy, *Talbot's Box* (1979); Frank McGuinness, *Observe the Sons of Ulster Marching Towards the Somme* (1985); Marina Carr, *On Raftery's Hill* (2000).

Given the existence of these Irish tragedies, we must reject Eagleton's assertion that 'It is interesting ... that there is very little tragic literature in this historically disrupted nation'.[13]

3

If tragedy can be written in the modern world, then *a fortiori* modern writers can appropriate Athenian tragedies. It is indeed the case that much European drama is based on the tragedies of Aeschylus, Sophocles, and Euripides; as Steiner says, 'The history of Western drama, as we know it, often reads like a prolonged echo of doomed informalities (literally the failure to define separate forms) between gods and men in a small number of Greek households'.[14] For Yeats points out that 'a great piece of literature is entirely of its own locality and yet infinitely translatable'.[15] In 1900, Joyce decided that this process had come to an end: 'It may be a vulgarism, but it is literal truth to say that Greek drama is played out ... Its revival is not of dramatic but of pedagogic significance'.[16] But in the case of modern drama, this judgement has proved to be disastrously wrong – as a brief look at plays produced in America, in England, and in France will serve to establish.[17]

In America, the topic of sex is stressed in two modern adaptations of Athenian tragedies. The themes of sexual repression and the Oedipus complex are emphasized in Eugene O'Neill's *Mourning Becomes Electra* (1931), which transfers Aeschylus' *Oresteia* to New England in the nineteenth century (though without its final resolution and religious theme). In his *Medea*, Robinson Jeffers shows how the beautiful Medea is turned into an avenging Fury when she is sexually abandoned by Jason. Ezra Pound, who did so much to put literary translation on the map, translated Sophocles' *Women of Trachis* (1956) and *Elektra* (1990).[18] Attracted by the non-naturalistic nature of the *Women of Trachis* (which makes it akin to the Japanese Noh), Pound rightly stresses the plot that deals with the unintended death of Herakles at the hands of his wife Deianeira, and leads nonetheless to a kind of cosmic order: 'WHAT SPLENDOUR IT ALL COHERES'. Pound's translation admirably captures the dialogue of Sophocles – as that between Herakles and Hyllus – and provides a rich orchestration of the choral odes. Written together with Rudd Fleming, Pound's translation of *Elektra* examines the question of where justice lies amid the conflicting claims of people to be right, and finds the key phrase of the play to be Elektra's question to her sister: 'Need we add cowardice to all the rest of this filth?'

In modern England, both translations and loose adaptations of Athenian tragedies were produced. Significant were the translations by Sir Richard Jebb and by Gilbert Murray: Jebb's translations of Sophocles (used by Yeats for his Oedipus plays) have recently been called 'still the most reliable and nuanced English translations of Sophocles';[19] Murray's rhymed translations of Euripides (which now seem very dated) sold more than 250,000 copies by 1920. More recently, Tony Harrison, who has a degree in Greek and Latin from Leeds University, has vigorously translated Aeschylus' *Oresteia* into a version of Anglo-Saxon English.

The foremost exemplar in England of how to appropriate Athenian tragedies in loose adaptations set in the modern age is T.S. Eliot, five of whose plays relate to a Greek original: *Murder in the Cathedral* (1935) to *Agamemnon*; *The Family Reunion* (1939) to

The Libation-Bearers; *The Cocktail Party* (1950) to *Alcestis*; *The Confidential Clerk* (1953) to *Ion*; and *The Elder Statesman* (1958) to *Oedipus at Colonus*. Eliot's technique can be seen from the fact that in *The Cocktail Party* he has realized by Act 1, scene iii the situation achieved at the end of *Alcestis* – the return of Alcestis from the dead – and then goes on to deal with what happens next; at the same time, Eliot doubles particular roles so that Alcestis becomes both Lavinia *and* Celia.[20] But it is doubtful that these etiolated plays will last.

But the country that has, until recently, produced the most remarkable body of plays that appropriate Athenian tragedies in various ways is France:[21] Gide's *Oedipus* (1931) and *Philoctetes* (1899); Cocteau's *Antigone* (1922) and *The Infernal Machine*, based on King Oedipus (1934); Giraudoux's *The Trojan War Will Not Take Place* (1935) and *Electra* (1937); Sartre's *The Flies*, based on the *Oresteia* (1943); Anouihl's *Antigone* (1942) and *Medea* (1946). These plays often make anachronistic use of modern material, which can render them both real and comic: in Giraudoux's *Electra*, we find cigars and coffee; in Anouilh's *Medea*, Medea becomes a foul-mouthed Russian gypsy. Then a striking feature of some of these plays is the distancing effect that the use of Greek myth brings about (as it already did in fifth century Athens). So Anouilh's *Antigone* and Sartre's *The Flies*, which were staged in Paris during the Nazi occupation and the Vichy government, can deal with the theme of resistance to tyranny without appearing to do so. So too Giraudoux's *The Trojan War Will Not Take Place* of 1935, which is essentially a prelude to the *Iliad*, suggests the coming war in Europe.

4

Hall has recently asserted that 'More Greek tragedy has been performed in the last thirty years than at any point in history since Greco-Roman antiquity'.[22] Frank McGuinness concurs:[23] 'It seems to be happening through the English-speaking world, that the Greeks are emerging as the dominant international force in our theatre' (and indeed elsewhere). The fact that Greek tragedies very often depict a clash of value systems chimes with the movement, from the late 1960s on, from a traditional, authoritarian set of values to a modern, radical set of values. Indeed the removal of certainties in a partly post-Christian world ensures that the uncertainties of Greek tragedy become a major resource; as Camus said,[24] tragedy can be produced at a time of transition 'between a sacred society and a society built by men'. Colin Teevan concurs:[25]

> One of the reasons for this resurgence of interest in Greek tragedy in the last 10 to 15 years, I would argue, is the fact that we are living in what we might call a post-Christian age. In Greek drama, there is no set right and wrong, no definitive answers or moral high ground. In a world where we are re-examining moral questions that at one time would have been taken for granted, Greek drama is of particular relevance.

The movement away from certainties has been specially pronounced in Ireland, where, from the 1960s on, a major clash was enacted between traditional, almost Victorian values and modernity, if not postmodernism:[26] it could indeed be argued that Ireland moved, at breakneck speed, from being a Victorian society to being a postmodern one, without an intervening modern period. In this very volatile situation, Greek tragedy allows for the exploration of issues of nationalism, of gender, of resistance to authority, of questioning of religion (especially the Roman Catholic Church).

The position of modern Irish dramatists is further complicated by Ireland's position as a postcolonial country,[27] not least in regard to language. While it is true that, in postcolonial societies, the loss of an indigenous language (such as Irish) may seem traumatic, it is also true that writers in such a society can appropriate the language of the colonizer to great effect, so that they appear to endorse the slave Caliban's statement to Prospero in *The Tempest*: 'You taught me language and my profit on't/Is, I know how to curse' (1.2.362-3). Hence Heaney asserts that 'English is by now not so much an imperial humiliation as a native weapon',[28] a significant example of which in the plays considered here is the use of the Midland dialect of Hiberno-English in Marina Carr's tragedies *By the Bog of Cats...* (based on *Medea*) and *Ariel* (based on *Oresteia*).

5

It is time to attempt an overview of Irish appropriation of Athenian tragedy.[29] First of all, a list of the plays in question:

Irish Plays Based on Greek Tragedies

Aeschylus:

Edward & Christine Longford	***The Oresteia*** (1935)
Louis MacNeice	***Agamemnon*** (1936)

| Tom Murphy | *The Sanctuary Lamp* (1975) – based on *Oresteia* |
| Tom Paulin | *Seize the Fire* (1990) – based on *Prometheus Bound* |

Sophocles:

J.M. Synge	*The Playboy of the Western World* (1907) – based on *King Oedipus*
W.B. Yeats	*King Oedipus* (1926)
W.B. Yeats	*Oedipus at Colonus* (1927)
Sydney B. Smith	*Sherca* (1979) – based on *Philoctetes*
Aidan Mathews	*Antigone* (1984)
Tom Paulin	*The Riot Act* (1985) – based on *Antigone*
Brendan Kennelly	*Antigone* (1986)
Seamus Heaney	*The Cure at Troy* (1990) – based on *Philoctetes*
Frank McGuinness	*Electra* (1997)
Desmond Egan	*Philoctetes* (1998)
Mary Elizabeth Burke-Kennedy	*Oedipus* (2000) – based on *King Oedipus*
Conall Morrison	*Antigone* (2003)
Seamus Heaney	*The Burial at Thebes* (2004) – based on *Antigone*
Eamon Grennan & Rachel Kitzinger	*Oedipus at Colonus* (2005)

Euripides:

George Bernard Shaw	*Major Barbara* (1905) – based on *Bacchae*
Brian Friel	*Living Quarters* (1978) – based on *Hippolytus*
Brendan Kennelly	*Medea* (1988)
Desmond Egan	*Medea* (1991)
Derek Mahon	*The Bacchae* (1991)
Ulick O'Connor	*The Oval Machine* – based on *Hippolytus*
Brendan Kennelly	*The Trojan Women* (1993)
Aidan Mathews	*Trojans* (1995)
Marina Carr	*By the Bog of Cats ...* (1998) – based on *Medea*
Colin Teevan	*Iph...* (1999) – based on *Iphigeneia in Aulis*
Colin Teevan	*Bacchae* (2002)
Edna O'Brien	*Iphigenia* (2003) – based on *Iphigeneia in Aulis*
Frank McGuinness	*Hecuba* (2004)

This list establishes that only a limited number of Athenian tragedies are used by Irish writers, but that certain plays are very popular indeed. In the case of Aeschylus, six Irish plays relate to the *Oresteia* and one to *Prometheus Bound* (which is probably not by Aeschylus); no plays relate to *Persians*, *Seven Against Thebes*, *Suppliants*. In the case of Sophocles, five plays relate to *Antigone*, three to *King Oedipus* and to *Philoctetes*, two to *Oedipus at Colonus* and one to *Electra*; no play relates to *Ajax* or *Women of Trachis*. In the case of Euripides, three plays relate to *Medea*, while two relate to *Bacchae*, *Hippolytus*, *Trojan Women* and *Iphigeneia in Aulis*; and one to *Hecuba*. No play relates to the tragicomedies *Alcestis*, *Iphigeneia in Tauris*, *Ion*, and *Helen*, or to the tragedies *Andromache*, *Children of Herakles*, *Herakles*, *Electra*, *Orestes*, *Phoenician Women*, *Suppliants*. The result of all this is that twenty-four Irish plays derive from *Oresteia*, *Antigone*, *King Oedipus*, *Philoctetes*, *Medea*, *Bacchae*.

It is important to understand the dynamics lying behind the process of using Athenian tragedies. We tend to glibly employ terms such as 'tradition', 'influence', legacy', 'heritage' when we are talking about the use made by modern writers of Greek material. But the metaphors involved in those terms suggest a *passive* process, whereas, from the point of view of the modern writer, the process is, rather, *active*. As Eliot said, 'mature poets steal'.[30] Marina Carr concurs: 'It seems that you are allowed to steal what you need while learning the craft and that there is no crime in that'.[31] The process is well described by the verb 'appropriate', meaning, according to the OED, 'to make over to anyone as their own'.

A further useful metaphor to describe this process of using Athenian tragedies is provided by the Brazilian concept of 'cannibalism',[32] in which the colonized people *devour* the material from the colonists 'in a new purified and energized form that is appropriate to the needs of the native peoples'.[33] So the colonized Irish devour Athenian tragedies to a spectacular extent, but this form of postcolonial translation is of a very complex nature. In the case of most former colonies, the postcolonial translation in question is from the native language of the colony into the homogenizing language of the colonizer (with a view to an international audience); this is often into 'the one master-language of our postcolonial world, English'.[34] But in postcolonial Ireland, the situation is much more elaborate.[35] Certainly, there is translation from Irish, the language of the colonized, into English, the language of the colonizer. But this linguistic process does not arise in the case of Irish writers who have abandoned Irish and themselves write in English. So when Irish writers produce translations of Athenian tragedies in their mother tongue English, the postcolonial comes in not at the level of *language* – because their language is the international language – but at the level of *culture*. Hence the twenty-six Irish appropriations of Athenian tragedy that date from 1975 onwards are deeply implicated in the movement in Ireland from a homogenous Victorian society to a modern, if not post-modern, heterogeneous society.

6

Three features of Irish appropriation of Athenian tragedies should be noted: the various ways the Irish plays relate to the original; the strong stress on Sophocles' plays; and the great emphasis on the experience of women.

The transposition of the source text (an Athenian tragedy) in the source language (Greek) to a target text (an Irish tragedy) in the target language (English) involves one of three manoeuvres: straight interlingual translation; version; loose adaptation. In this process restrictions operate: the *area* is restricted to transportation from Greek to English; the *time* is restricted to a movement from fifth century Athens to modern Ireland; and the *text type* is restricted to the use of Athenian tragedies to generate Irish tragedies.[36] These translations of plays are of the utmost importance: as de Stael says, 'If translations of poems enrich literature, translations of plays could exert an even greater influence, for the theatre is truly literature's executive power'.[37]

In the case of straight translation, the Irish translator may have a perfect knowledge of both the source language (Greek) and the target language (English) – as with the Longfords (*Oresteia*), Louis MacNeice (*Agamemnon*), and Desmond Egan (*Medea* and *Philoctetes*). These authors provide a faithful, but not literal translation, aiming for dynamic equivalence, what Dryden called 'paraphrase'. Such straight translations are, paradoxically, radical, because they force the reader or viewer to envisage what the original Athenian tragedy meant in its own time. Furthermore, straight translations are essential for *teaching* purposes, for courses in Greek tragedy in Classical Civilization programmes (versions or loose adaptations are here a distraction).

In the case of a version, the Irish playwright preserves the *invariant core*[38] of the Athenian tragedy – Oedipus must kill his father and marry his mother – but feels free to add to, subtract from, manipulate the original. As Cowley said of his versions of Pindar's *Odes*, I have 'taken, left out and added what I please', what Dryden called 'imitation'.[39] So Kennelly's version of *Medea* keeps to the plot-line of Euripides' tragedy, but adds a very considerable amount of material that has a feminist slant.

In the case of loose adaptation, the Irish dramatist changes the setting to that of the modern world, but preserves some of the plot-line of the Athenian original as a kind of sub-text; as Ellmann writes of Joyce: 'the Homeric myth hovers behind Bloom in *Ulysses*, insistently altering the context of that book'.[40] So Marina Carr's play *By the Bog of Cats...* uses much of the plot of *Medea*, but transfers the setting to the contemporary Irish Midlands. We see, then, that a single Athenian play – Euripides' *Medea* – can generate a straight translation from Desmond Egan, a version from Brendan Kennelly, and a loose adaptation by Marina Carr.

7

Writing in 1996, Fitzgerald notes 'The popularity of Euripides in classical scholarship over the past thirty years', and the fact that 'Sophocles has become a silent presence'.[41] This has not been the case for Irish writers, who have, since 1979, produced eleven translations, versions, and loose adaptations of Sophocles. So the question arises: why this stress on Sophocles? One answer is the sheer quality of the seven tragedies we possess, and the likely quality of the very numerous lost plays; as Yeats said, 'we might, had the total works of Sophocles survived ... not think him (Shakespeare) greatest'.[42] A further answer is that, when we say that tragedy can still be written by someone like Beckett, it is because he can be compared with Sophocles:

> Beckett himself gives us a drama that is remarkably Sophoclean: the tensed economy of the stage action, the impossibility of defining precisely questions of guilt and responsibility, the bitter-sweet combination of cruelty and gentleness, and above all, the ritual power of ordinary language are features which cannot be found in precisely this way outside the Western theatre, and which were put there by the Greek ancestors of the line.[43]

But a further, crucial factor in Sophocles' dominance is the stress in his work on the theme of *recognition* (what Aristotle called *anagnorisis*) and the resonances of that theme in the post-colonial Republic of Ireland and the semi-colonial Northern Ireland. Sophocles' stress on characters who fail to achieve recognition and do not perceive the nature of reality finds its objective correlative in the two Irish societies: while it is essential for these societies (as well as the colonial power, England) that they know themselves because of a history of colonial dependence, they may well fail to achieve this self-knowledge. Hence Irish *Antigones* show how both the Northern and Southern States are deluded in their attempts to suppress the individual person; for neither the Unionist Creon of Paulin's *The Riot Act*, nor the Republic of Ireland in Matthew's *Antigone* possess self-knowledge.

8

In appropriations of Greek tragedies by Irish writers, there is a great stress on the experience of women as embodied in powerful female characters. Five plays deal with Antigone, a woman who opposes the male ruler Creon; three plays present Medea, arguably the first feminist; further plays give us Electra, determined avenger of her father, Hecuba, equally determined avenger of her son Polydorus, and Iphigeneia, sacrificed for the Greeks; two plays deal with the female worshippers of Dionysus, and two with the captured Women of Troy. This great stress on the experience of women clearly relates to what happened to women in modern Ireland.

The position of women in Ireland during the course of the twentieth century changed greatly. From about 1820 to 1960, Irish women had to contend with a patriarchal system that was deeply authoritarian. To a large extent, women were excluded from the male worlds of politics and of work. Because there was no contraception, they were often forced to have large numbers of children, and they, like men, suffered that peculiar form of sexual repression that arose initially out of the economies of the small farm in the nineteenth century.

The opening up of Ireland from 1960 on to a wide variety of external influences had large consequences for women. They could now work on equal terms with men, gradually began to play a greater part in politics, and became better educated. Women were also enabled to take charge of their sexual behaviour because contraception was legalized. Nevertheless, there was a sense that much remained to be done for women, art being one sphere of activity which could highlight this. So a number of male playwrights made a conscious decision to enact the ongoing drama about the position of women in Ireland by appropriating Greek tragedies that had done the same 2,500 years earlier. The most explicit connection between the conditions of Irish society and Athenian drama is made by Brendan Kennelly: 'The ancient, original Greek infiltrates life in modern Ireland'.[44]

So while the Athenian tragedians portrayed powerful women in a way that bore no relation to the actual lives of women in fifth-century Athens, and used women characters to explore contradictions in their own society, Irish male playwrights reflect a society in which women have increasingly come to enjoy various types of freedom, and set out to advocate further power for women. As the Chorus says in both Euripides' *Medea* and Kennelly's *Medea*, 'There will be/womansongs in the answer to the false/songs of men'.[45]

The programme for women that emerges in these Irish plays includes the following: women are to be independent and free from restraint; women must set out both to change men and to usurp the role of men in the world; women must react to their oppression with rage. For the male playwright, the aim in all of this is, as Kennelly says, 'to be imaginatively a woman'.[46] As a result, 'it is not the gendered identity of the translator as such which influences the politics of transmission as much as the *project* which the translator is promoting'.[47]

9

In a world where very few people, however well educated, know classical Greek, the translation or adaptation of paradigmatic Athenian tragedies becomes an intellectual and artistic imperative. The reason this imperative has been so eagerly seized upon by important Irish playwrights and poets is that 'Ireland has the last English-speaking contemporary drama that still sees the theatre as the natural place to juggle ideas'.[48] So Irish writers who appropriate Athenian tragedies do not simply bear witness to a glorious past, but seek actively to comment on the present and to shape a future.[49] In so doing, Irish writers provide a particular gloss on Pearse's idea that Ireland should be a new Greece: 'What the Greek was to the ancient world, the Gael will be to the modern'.[50]

---

[1] Milton, Preface to *Samson Agonistes*; P. Ricoeur, *The Symbolism of Evil* (Boston: 1969), p. 221; Virginia Woolf, *The Common Reader* (London: Hogarth Press, 1925; *Letters on Poetry from W.B. Yeats to Dorothy Wellesley* (London: Oxford University Press, 1964), p. 194.

[2] For Leavis on Shakespeare see I. McKillop, *F.R. Leavis: A Life in Criticism* (London: Penguin, 1995), pp. 174-77.

[3] Jorge Louis Borges, *The Aleph* (London: Longman, 1998), pp. 69-78.

[4] G. Steiner, *The Death of Tragedy* (New Haven/London: Yale University Press, 1996); M. Weitz, quoted in *Tragedy*, eds. J. Drakakis and N.C. Liebler (London: Longman, 1998), p. 3.

[5] Aristophanes, *The Frogs* 949-52; Horace, *Ars Poetica* 95-8.

[6] For tragedy and the novel see T. Eagleton, *Sweet Violence – The Idea of the Tragic* (Oxford: Blackwell, 2003), pp. 178-202.

[7] Balzac, quoted in Eagleton (note 6), p. 93.

[8] J. Orr, *Tragic Drama and Modern Society* (London: Longman 1981), p. xvii.

[9] T.R. Henn, *The Harvest of Tragedy* (London: Methuen, 1966), pp. 197-216.

[10] C. Leech, *Tragedy* (London: Methuen, 1969), p. 26.

[11] L. Pilkington, *Theatre and the State in Twentieth Century Ireland* (London: Routledge, 2001), pp. 99-102; C. Morash, *A History of Irish Theatre 1601-2000* (Cambridge: Cambridge University Press, 2002), pp. 163-71.

[12] For modern Irish drama see A. Roche, *Contemporary Irish Drama* (Dublin: Gill & Macmillan, 1994); C. Murray, *Twentieth-Century Irish Drama* (Manchester: Manchester University Press, 1997); N. Grene, *The Politics of Irish Drama* (Cambridge: Cambridge University Press, 1999); Pilkington (note 11); Morash (note 11).

[13] Eagleton (note 6), p. 304.

[14] G. Steiner, *After Babel* (Oxford: Oxford University Press, 1998), p. 477. For translation see, in addition to Steiner, *On Translation*, ed. R.A. Brower (New York: Oxford University Press, 1966); S. Bassnett-McGuire, *Translation Studies* (London: Routledge, 1991); *Translation/History/Culture*, ed. A. Lefevere (London: Routledge, 1992); J. Munday, *Introducing Translation Studies* (London: Routledge, 2002).

[15] W.B. Yeats in E.H. Mikhail, ed., *W.B. Yeats: Interviews and Recollections*, vol. ii (London: Macmillan, 1977), pp. 199-203.

[16] James Joyce, *Occasional, Critical, and Political Writing*, ed. K. Barry (Oxford: Oxford University Press, 2000), p. 23.

[17] K. von Fritz, *Antike und Moderne Tragodie*, 1962; L. Aylen, *Greek Tragedy and the Modern World* (London: Longman, 1964); A. Belli, *Ancient Greek Myths and Modern Drama* (London: Longman, 1969).

[18] H.A. Mason, 'The Women of Trachis and Creative Translation' in *Ezra Pound*, ed. J.P. Sullivan (Harmondsworth: Penguin, 1970), pp. 279-310; P. Reid, 'Introduction' in *Sophocles Elektra* by Ezra Pound and R. Fleming (London: Faber & Faber, 1990), pp. ix-xx.

[19] S. Goldhill in *The Cambridge Companion to Greek Tragedy*, ed. P.E. Easterling (Cambridge: Cambridge University Press, 1997), p. 330.

[20] For Eliot's Greek-based plays see R.G. Tanner, *Greece and Rome* 17(1970), pp. 123-34.

[21] For these French plays see G. Highet, *The Classical Tradition* (Oxford: Oxford University Press, 1967), pp. 520-40; Aylen (note 17), pp. 258-311; M.L. Blanchard, *Modern Drama* 29(1986), pp. 41-48.

[22] E. Hall in *Dionysus Since 69 – Greek Tragedy at the Dawn of the Third Millennium*, eds. E. Hall, F. Macintosh and A. Wrigley (Oxford: Oxford University Press, 2005), p. 2. At pp. 1-46, Hall answers the question 'Why Greek Tragedy in the Late Twentieth Century?'

23 Frank McGuinness, Interview with J. Long in *Amid Our Troubles – Irish Versions of Greek Tragedy*, eds. M. McDonald and J.M. Walton (London: Methuen, 2002), p. 280.

24 Camus, quoted in Hall (note 22), p. 44.

25 Colin Teevan, Interview with S. Lynch, *The Irish Times* 20/8/2005.

26 For Ireland as postmodern see D. Bell in *Across the Frontiers: Ireland in the 1990s*, ed. R. Kearney (Dublin: Wolfhound Press, 1988), pp. 228-29.

27 For Ireland as postcolonial see J. Macleod, *Beginning Postcolonialism* (Manchester: Manchester University Press, 2000), pp. 240-46; for postcolonial drama see H. Gilbert and J. Tompkins, *Post-Colonial Drama* (London: Routledge, 1996); for postcolonialism in Irish drama see D. Duncan, *Postcolonial Theory in Irish Drama from 1800-2000* (Lewiston: Mellen Press, 2004).

28 Seamus Heaney, quoted in J. Haffenden, *Yearbook of English Studies* 17(1987), p. 115.

29 For these Irish plays see esp. McDonald and Walton (note 23); also F. Macintosh, *Dying Acts – Death in Ancient Greek and Modern Irish Tragic Drama* (Cork: Cork Univeristy Press, 1994); B. Arkins, *Hellenising Ireland: Greek and Roman Themes in Modern Irish Literature* (Newbridge: Goldsmith Press, 2005), pp. 143-73; *Rebel Women – Staging Ancient Greek Drama Today*, eds. J. Dillon and S.E. Wilmer (London: Methuen, 2005), pp. 115-73.

30 T.S. Eliot, *Selected Essays* (New York: Faber & Faber, 1964), p. 182.

31 Marina Carr, *Irish University Review* 28(1998), p. 196.

32 E.R.P. Vieira in *Post-Colonial Translation*, ed. S. Bassnett and H. Trivedi (London: Routledge, 1999), pp. 95-113.

33 Munday (note 14), p. 136.

34 S. Bassnett and H. Trivedi in Bassnett-Trivedi (note 32), 13.

35 M. Cronin, *Translating Ireland: Translation, Languages, Culture* (Cork: Cork University Press, 1996); My. Tymoczko, *Translation in a Post-Colonial Context: Early Irish Literature in English Translation* (Manchester: Manchester University Press, 1999).

36 Munday (note 14), p. 12.

37 de Stael, quoted in *Translation/History/Culture*, ed. A. Lefevere (London: Routledge, 1992), p. 18.

38 For 'the invariant core' see Bassnett-McGuire (note 14), p. 18, p. 22, pp. 26-27, p. 87.

39 Cowley, quoted in Munday (note 26), p. 24.

40 R. Ellmann, *James Joyce* (Oxford: Oxford University Press, 1983), p.4.

41 G. Fitzgerald, *Ramus* 25(1996), p. 12.

42 W.B. Yeats, *A Vision* (London: T. Werner Laurie, 1925), p. 204.

43 T.G. Rosenmeyer in *The Legacy of Greece*, ed. M.I. Finley (Oxford: Oxford University Press, 1981), p. 123; for Beckett and Greek Tragedy see K. Worth in Hall, Macintosh and Wrigley (note 22), pp. 265-83.

44 Brendan Kennelly, *Antigone* (Newcastle-upon-Tyne: Bloodaxe, 1996), p. 51.

45 Brendan Kennelly, *Medea* (Newcastle-upon-Tyne: Bloodaxe, 1991), p. 34.

[46] Cf. R. Pine in *Dark Fathers into Light: Brendan Kennelly*, ed. R. Pine (Newcastle-upon-Tyne: Bloodaxe, 1994), p. 22.

[47] S. Simon, *Gender in Translation* (London: Routledge, 1996), pp. viii-ix; for women in contemporary Irish drama see R. Pelan in *(Post) Colonial Stages*, ed. H. Gilbert (Yorkshire: Dangeroo, 1999), pp. 243-52.

[48] J.M. Walton in *Amid Our Troubles* (note 23), p. 8.

[49] Cronin (note 27).

[50] Pearse, quoted in Macintosh (note 29), p. 1.

3 | Sophocles' *Antigone*

Sophocles' tragedy *Antigone*,[1] which was produced about the year 441 BC, deals with the situation that exists in Thebes after the king Oedipus, found guilty of parricide and incest, is deposed from the throne. At some stage, Oedipus curses his two sons – Eteocles ('True Fame') and Polyneices ('Much Strife') – who end up quarrelling about which of them should be king of Thebes. Polyneices determines that he will seize the throne, and goes to Argos, where the king Adrastus organizes a body of troops to attack Thebes and make Polyneices king (this is often referred to as the Seven Against Thebes, as in Aeschylus' play of that name). In the subsequent battle between the forces of Argos and Thebes (won by Thebes), Polyneices and Eteocles kill each other in accordance with their father's curse. Eteocles is given full burial rites as a loyal defender of Thebes, but the new king Creon, who is largely portrayed in *Antigone* as a tyrant, forbids the burial of Polyneices because he is a traitor. Polyneices' sister Antigone defies Creon's edict in order to bury her brother (an act that makes her liable to death by stoning); her sister Ismene refuses to help. Sophocles' play focuses on the resulting clash between Creon and Antigone in a way that seems to be mainly his own invention.

To understand *Antigone*, it is important to be aware of how vital proper funeral rites, including burial, were thought to be in Greek religion.[2] For the Greeks (as for the Irish), death was not regarded as a single, instantaneous event, but was, rather, conceived of as a process lasting about a month, in which women played a significant role. After the woman of the house had washed, anointed and dressed the body of the dead person, ritual mourning followed for two days, while on the third day the funeral procession and burial took place, to be followed by a ritual meal. Offerings were made at the tomb of the dead person on the ninth and thirtieth days after death. In all of this, what was of paramount importance was the provision of a proper burial for the dead person, so that he or she could be at peace in the after life, would not have to suffer dishonour, and would not bring down the anger of the gods upon the living.

Already in Homer's *Iliad*, burial is an issue: the king of Troy Priam goes to the Greek warrior Achilles, who has dishonoured the body of his son Hector, in order to get back the body for proper funeral rites; Achilles agrees to return the body. During a battle in 424 BC in the Peloponnesian War between Athens and Sparta, the victorious Boeotians refused to hand over the Athenian dead for burial, and this event may have prompted the situation in Euripides' tragedy *The Suppliant Women*, in which the Thebans refuse to allow the burial of the Argive warriors. Then in Sophocles' play *Ajax*, the Greek leaders forbid the burial of Ajax because he is viewed as an enemy.

In Sophocles' *Antigone*, Antigone is determined that her brother will have a proper burial, and she duly performs the basic funeral rite of placing dust on Polyneices' body. Indeed Antigone is (together with Electra) the most intransigent of Sophocles' heroes: nothing at all can change her resolve. Her defiant act leads to a series of disastrous consequences. When Creon finds out what Antigone has done, he has her immured alive in a cave (instead of stoned). Three suicides follow: that of Antigone who hangs herself (the usual mode of suicide for women in tragedy);[3] that of Haemon, betrothed to Antigone, who kills himself with a sword; and that of Eurydice, wife of Creon, who also kills herself with a sword. Creon, though alive, speaks of himself as dead.

The clash between Creon and Antigone can usefully be analysed in terms of the binary oppositions of structuralism. Creon is an old man; Antigone is a young woman. Creon is a representative of the city (*polis*) and of the community; Antigone is a representative of the individual person and of the family. Creon is a champion of statute law (*nomos*); Antigone is a champion of nature (*physis*). Creon is indifferent to the gods of the underworld; Antigone is an upholder of the gods of the underworld. Creon favours the living; Antigone favours the dead.

This clash between Creon and Antigone raises the question as to which of them is right, and that question is not left unresolved in *Antigone*: the blind prophet Teiresias, who 'has never spoken a falsehood to the city' (line 1094), comes down without equivocation on the side of Antigone, on the side of the unwritten laws of the gods that require proper burial for Polyneices. So Antigone can go to her death unrepentant, while Creon is forced to admit that he was wrong, and help in the burial of Polyneices. Antigone can therefore be seen as a female intruder[4] into the male world, who, like Medea and Lysistrata, causes major disruption in that world.

2

For more than two centuries, Sophocles' *Antigone* has been the most valued of all the Athenian tragedies. *Antigone* was given important, though partial, readings by the major figures of Hegel, Hölderlin and Kierkegaard[5] in the early nineteenth century; the later nineteenth century saw a very influential production of *Antigone*; and in the twentieth century, *Antigone* became the paradigmatic play for exploring the clash between a repressive state and the individual person.

Hegel's reading of *Antigone* fits into his general positivism, his belief that historical and political life move from crisis to crisis involving tragic destruction, but that also leads on to a richer, more productive stage in human life. So Hegel asserts that *both* Creon *and* Antigone are right; that both of them are destroyed, since Antigone dies and Creon is a living dead man; and that in the end the city of Thebes will accommodate Antigone's principles. That Antigone and Creon are destroyed is beyond doubt, but Hegel is wrong to regard Creon, whom he terms on ethical principle (*ein ethisches Prinzip*) as being justified, and wrong to find a positive message in the roll-call of death at the end of the play.

For Hölderlin, Antigone is a very impatient human being who cannot wait to avenge the wrong done to her brother Polyneices: since the gods are slow to act, she must be quick. Partial justification for this reading could come from the concept that the first burial of Polyneices was divine, while the second burial was by an Antigone unwilling to wait for the gods to complete the task.

Dwelling on the sorrow of human life and referring to himself in his diaries as 'Antigone', Kierkegaard places Antigone, the daughter and sister of Oedipus, in absolute solitude which she does not wish to abandon in order to marry Haemon. Accordingly, Antigone provokes a crisis with Creon, so that she can die and be with the only person on earth who is like her, Oedipus. This reading blithely ignores Antigone's overwhelming desire to bury her brother, her immense thirst for justice.

In the second half of the nineteenth century, what did most to keep *Antigone* in the public view as a landmark production of the play in a translation by Johann Donner and with music by Mendelssohn.[6] Premiering in Potsdam in 1841, this *Antigone* went to Paris (1844), London (1845), Edinburgh, Athens (1867), and Moscow (1899), giving the lie to Matthew Arnold's assertion of 1853 that 'it is no longer possible that we should feel a deep interest in the *Antigone* of Sophocles'.[7]

In the twentieth century, to read *Antigone* in terms of conflict between a repressive State and the individual person has been immensely productive. In Poland, where there were four productions of *Antigone* in the period 1962-65, Andrei Hadya's *Antigone* of 1984, set in the Gdansk shipyard, linked the play to the Solidarity movement. In Athol Fugard's play *The Island* (1973), two political prisoners in apartheid South Africa find that *Antigone* is about themselves. The fall of the Greek Colonels in 1974 was marked by a production of *Antigone* in Athens. Less politically clear-cut was Anouilh's *Antigone*, which was staged in Nazi-occupied Paris in the winter of 1943-4, and appeared to give equal validity to Antigone and to Creon. But in the same circumstances, Sartre is very clear about the function of Greek drama: 'Why stage declamatory Greeks ... unless to disguise what one was thinking under a fascist regime?'

When it comes to appropriating Sophocles' *Antigone*, Ireland will not be found wanting: there are versions by Tom Paulin (*The Riot Act*); Brendan Kennelly (*Antigone*); Conall Morrison (*Antigone*); and Seamus Heaney (*The Burial at Thebes*); and there is a loose adaptation by Aidan Mathews (*Antigone*).[8] Analysis of these follows after a brief interlude.

3

It is not the purpose of this book to dwell on the problems of translating the Greek of Athenian dramatists into English, but it is worth analysing briefly one difficulty that arises in the famous second Choral Ode of *Antigone*,[9] in order to show that translation can never be an exact science. Sophocles here draws on the privileging of Man by the Sophists to describe human control over

the environment – over the sea, animals and birds – but this
control proves ambivalent, because the sea is later linked to
irrational suffering, because the behaviour of animals and birds
indicates that divine order has been violated, and because man is
subject to death. Ambivalent, too, is the behaviour of man in the
areas of law and justice, men capable, like Creon, of being
irrational, destructive, tyrannical.

How then are we to translate the opening statement of the
Chorus (lines 332-33)? A typical translation is 'There are many
wonders in the world,/But none is more wonderful than man'.[10] But
while the Greek adjective *deinos* can mean 'wonderful' (and, in its
plural, 'wonders'), it can also mean 'terrible', 'powerful', 'clever',
and words similar in meaning to these.[11] The difficulty lies in
deciding which of these meanings best fits the context, or indeed
whether more than one meaning should be used. In view of the
ambivalence about men in *Antigone*, the use of the adjective
'wonderful' does not seem to be appropriate. Better is Lloyd-Jones's
adjective 'formidable' because that term does suggest an element of
the awesome. Indeed Sommerstein uses this adjective 'awesome'.[12]
But the best strategy seems to be to employ two English words to
translate *deinos*: Grene and Lattimore have 'Many the wonders but
nothing walks stronger than men'; Fagles has 'Numberless
wonders/terrible wonders walk the world but none the match for
man'.[13]

The Irish versions of *Antigone* do not advance beyond
'wonderful' and 'wonders': Paulin has 'There are many wonders on
this earth/and man has made the most of them'; Kennelly has
'Wonders are many/and none is more wonderful than man';
Morrison has 'The world has many wonders,/but none so
marvellous as man'; Heaney has 'Among the many wonders of the
World/Where is the equal of this creature, man?'[14]

4

The Irish versions of *Antigone* by Paulin, Mathews, Morrison and
Heaney deal in one way or another with the political theme: the
State versus the individual person. In Paulin, this conflict occurs in
Northern Ireland. When Civil Rights agitation broke out in
Northern Ireland in 1968, it was inevitable that the Antigone theme
would surface. Conor Cruise O'Brien[15] first held that 'civil
disobedience, in Northern Ireland, was likely to prove an effective
lever for social change', but was soon damning Antigone with faint

praise, and suggesting that she was responsible for the deaths of herself, her fiancé Haemon, and Creon's wife, Eurydice.

> It was Antigone's free decision, and that alone, which precipitated the tragedy. Creon's responsibility was the more remote one of having placed this tragic power in the hands of a headstrong child of Oedipus.[16]

But Sophocles shows us clearly that Antigone is right and that Creon is wrong, because the claims of nature and unwritten laws take precedence over the positive laws of the state. As Lloyd-Jones, Regius Professor of Greek at Oxford, pointed out, 'Tiresias makes it clear that Creon has offended against the law of gods'.[17]

Tom Paulin's play *The Riot Act*, which was staged by the Field Day Theatre Company in Derry in 1984, is a version of *Antigone* that subtly relates the action to contemporary Northern Ireland; as the dialect forms indicate: 'a complete eejit'; 'thin wee grievance'; 'ould bugger'.[18] Creon becomes a Unionist politician who represents British law and engages, in the modern way, in 'spin':[19]

> Mr. Chairman, Loyal citizens of Thebes, these recent months have indeed been a most distressing time for us all. It therefore gives me great pleasure to report that public confidence and order are now fully restored, and, if I may, I would further like to take this opportunity of thanking each and every one of you for your steadfastness and your exceptional loyalty.

Antigone becomes a Republican who must bury her dead brother, funerals carrying a special charge in the nationalist community in Northern Ireland: 'I must bury him ... He's my own brother'.[20] These people espouse two different kinds of loyalty: Creon is devoted to law and order, and to the politics of unionism (the phrase 'the big man' identifies him with the Rev. Ian Paisley); Antigone is devoted to family, kin and tribe. The result is a clash between alien laws and a native ethos; as Antigone says, 'Down in the dark earth/there's no law says,/"Break with your own kin, go lick the state"'. For chthonic forces antecedent to all human law are the touchstone of justice for Antigone and for the audience who 'will understand'.[21]

Despite his banal assertion that 'I shall be doing a very great deal of listening', Creon is an utterly intransigent person who could neither bend nor listen and becomes violent towards Antigone: 'Go on boys ... Bring out the dirty bitch and let's be rid of her'. But Antigone's epithet is 'wild',[22] an adjective that has powerful connotations in Hiberno-English such as 'exuberant', 'untamed', 'outside the system'. For Antigone, such rejection of the political system means that she will die, and do so by following the tradition of Republican martyrs.

But Creon is eventually forced to change his mind and achieve knowledge (*anagnorisis*). Since his assertion 'I changed it utterly' appropriates a crucial phrase from Yeats's poem 'Easter 1916' referring to the impact of the 1916 rising, we infer that Creon's Unionist viewpoint has altered to take account of the Republican position – as is made clear by his use of Antigone's register of language about his dead son Haemon ('my own wee man', and 'bairn'), and by the burying of Polyneices with 'green laurel leaves'.[23] But Paulin's poem 'Under Creon' establishes that his preferred state, though green, would have to find room for the genuine Dissenters in Northern Ireland in the late eighteenth century such as Henry Joy McCracken, James Hope, and Joseph Biggar.[24]

In formal terms, the verse of *The Riot Act* employs a very short line that ensures great rapidity, as in these remarks of Antigone to her sister Ismene:[25]

> I'll not persuade you.
> You won't link hands with me,
> not now, not ever.
> That's your nature.
> But I'll bury him
> and die for it,
> though I've hurt no one.
> My heart goes out
> and honours them, our dead.

Paulin's prose, on the other hand, is weighty and clichéd, as in the words of Creon quoted above.

In *The Riot Act*, Paulin radically modernizes the Choral Odes on Man and on Love: Man 'owns the universe, the stars,/sput satellites and great societies'; 'A bruised peach, blood-orange – a padded cell, a frazzled moth? aye, well, you've known love.'[26]

5

The version of *Antigone* by the theatre director Conall Morrison, reproduces the plot of Sophocles, but is given modern resonance by the initial stage direction[27] – 'A projection screen. A burnt-out car. Rubble' – and the fact that this screen provided images of the modern conflict in the Middle East between Israelis and Palestinians. This concept of a contemporary war mirrors the

conflict between Polyneices and Eteocles – the Seven against
Thebes – that occurred immediately before the clash between
Antigone and Creon. As the play goes on, the stage directions
continue to stress that violence and destruction are ongoing. The
chorus, a single man, 'dances and stamps on the burnt out car,
bashes it with a large stick and pours a can of petrol over it'. When
Antigone and Isme are to be immured, 'Socks are pulled over
Antigone and Ismene's heads and yards of gaffer tape are wrapped
around their heads and hands. They are dragged off'.

Morrison stresses the dispute between Creon and Antigone
about the concept of law (*nomos*). Ismene holds that 'Creon's word
is law./Creon is the law'. Later, the Chorus tell Creon that 'Your
word is law'. Creon, for his part, states that 'while I'm alive,/no
woman's law will rot this state', and that 'For better or worse, I
make the laws'. But Antigone problematizes Creon's law by calling
it 'His law!' and by asserting that 'This law was not proclaimed by
God/or the powers of the earth and under.'

Morrison uses an emphatic modern register of language, as in
this address by Tiresias to Creon:

> Do you still think I'm singing for my supper?
> In the shortest time,
> your house will fill with the sound
> of men and women retching with their grief,
> and every family, in every city with a fallen son,
> will curse your name in hate:
> your plague has caused the priest to run from the graveside
> and in his place now the happy rats and dogs preside.

The elevated register of language used in Greek tragedy does not
permit the obscenities found in the comedy of the same period (as
in Aristophanes), but Morrison uses English obscenity to
considerable effect: the Guard asserts that 'Fate fucks you in the
end', and Antigone, in a shocking passage that goes well beyond
Sophocles, employs that elemental Anglo-Saxon verb, about God:
'Where is God?/Answer me?/I honour him; he pisses on me./Fuck
God/FUCK GOD!'

6

Seamus Heaney's version of *Antigone*, which is entitled *The Burial
at Thebes*, also moves the play out of Ireland onto the world stage.
This is how Heaney views the conflict between Creon and Antigone:

> Creon puts it to the Chorus in these terms: either you are a
> patriot, a loyal citizen, and regard Antigone as an enemy of the

state because she does honour to her traitor brother, or else you
yourselves are traitors because you stand up for a woman who has
broken the law and defied my authority.[28]

Such a conflict mirrors, Heaney asserts, the contemporary issue of
Iraq:

Just as Creon forced the citizens of Thebes into an either/or
situation in relation to Antigone, the Bush administration in the
White House was using the same tactic to forward its argument
for war on Iraq.[29]

In 2004, *Antigone* still functions as paradigm for oppression by the
State.

Heaney preserves the invariant core of *Antigone* that sees
Antigone and Creon as powerful advocates of their respective
positions. Here is Creon after the first burial of Polyneices:[30]

The gods, you think, are going to attend
To this particular corpse? Preposterous.
Did they hide him under clay for his religion?
For coming to burn their colonnaded temples?
For attacking a city under their protection?
The gods, you think, will side with the likes of him?
Here's something else for you to think about.
For a good while now I have had reports
Of disaffected elements at work here.
A certain poisonous minority
Unready to admit the rule of law
And my law in particular.

But there are several ways in which Heaney makes his version of
Antigone less bleak than Sophocles. His title *The Burial at Thebes*
not only raises the central issue of Polyneices' burial, but also might
point out that that burial has taken place, and so show that
Antigone's desire to bury her brother has been realized. Then in the
Choral Ode on Man, the Chorus is more positive about human
beings than Sophocles:[31] they introduce the rhetorical question
(expecting the answer 'nowhere') 'Where is the equal of this
creature, man?'; they add the dictum of the Sophist Protagoras that
man is the 'measure of all things'; and, crucially, they omit all
reference to man's greatest obstacle Death: 'from Death alone he
will find no rescue' (Fagles).[32]

Heaney states that what he aimed at in *The Burial at Thebes* was
'to do a translation that actors could speak as plainly or intensely as
the occasion demanded, but still keep faith with the ritual formality
of the original'.[33] In formal terms, he generally uses three-beat and

four-beat lines (inspired by Eibhlin Dubh Ni Chonaill's lament, *Caoineadh Airt Uí Laoghaire*), and for Creon the more prosaic iambic pentameter. A feature of Heaney's language is his air of contemporary formulae that can be ironic or colloquial in impact. So in the opening scene of the play, Antigone states that 'This is law and order/In the land of good king Creon'. She attributes to Creon the assertion that 'Whoever isn't for us/Is against us in this case'; and she says to Ismene about the burial of Polyneices 'No. No. Broadcasted./Your cover-ups sicken me'.[34] Such ironic use of language is also found in the opening statement of Creon who says: 'My nerve's not going to fail', and 'The whole crew must close ranks'.[35] Then the colloquial language of cliché is specially suited to the Guard who reports the burial of Polyneices: 'So here I am, the old dog for the hard road'; '"You take the high road, I'll take the low road"'.[36] Finally, Heaney uses a Hiberno-English idiom to link Antigone to men in general: the Chorus note that, if a man acts illegally, 'He'll have put himself beyond the pale'; Creon finds that Antigone, by burying Polyneices, 'puts herself beyond the pale ...'[37]

7

Aidan Mathews's *Antigone* is a loose adaptation of Sophocles that moves the action into the modern world. In so doing, Mathews draws on Pirandello's discovery that the mimesis of reality can hardly be distinguished from the imitation of an imitation, that what is spurious may well constitute a genuine reality, that truth is indeterminate.[38] Accordingly, the character named the Critic says that 'what we're seeing here tonight ... seriously misrepresents a tremendous play.' Part of that misrepresentation concerns the metatheatrical way the main characters perceive themselves. Antigone allows that Sophocles' play 'is one of the foundation texts of Western culture', and notes that 'I've been playing this part for three thousand years' (well before Sophocles), but also asserts that 'I am in my ass the Princess Antigone', and that 'I represent ordinariness'. Ismene, who is pregnant (or is she?) and loaded down with domestic chores, is not content with the modest role she has in Sophocles: 'I want a part with some flesh and blood. I want a real role.' And Creon refuses to accept that he causes the death of Antigone: 'You want to be a martyr. You want me to have you killed! But I won't do it.' So in Mathews, Antigone does not die, but was 'seen in Kharkov only last year.'[39]

On the other hand, the serious side of the Sophoclean original is also represented. Antigone says to Creon: 'I ended up dead. You were deposed. Nothing was left.' And Antigone sees herself as a scapegoat who suffers for 'innocent victims' and 'guilty culprits' alike,[40] a theme treated in relation to Greek tragedy by Mathews's mentor René Girard (to whom his play is dedicated).[41] The violence of Sophocles' *Antigone* is also given its due. What corresponds to the war between Eteocles and Polyneices is a modern world that is devastated by war and that scarcely functions at all, so that Creon and Antigone agree that violence and death are 'the most natural things in the world'.[42]

This violence is found in contemporary Ireland because Mathews's play was written in the context of the Criminal Justice bill passed by the Dail in 1984, which gave more power to the Gardai (police) to seize and detain suspects. Described as 'draconian' and as showing a 'a loss of confidence in our system of law',[43] this Bill was handed out to the initial audience at the Project Arts Theatre in Dublin in 1984, and was played by Creon on tape during the play and at the interval. So the violence presided over by Creon's chief of police Heman (an ironic take on Haemon) is matched by erosion of civil liberty in contemporary Ireland. Hence temporal barriers break down: 'The drama is set in Ireland in the 1980s BC, soon after Sparta had entered the war on the German side.' The resulting violence leads Ismene and Creon to say: 'The best of us are unhinged by the horrors we have witnessed.'[44]

The core issue of Sophocles' *Antigone* appears in another form in Mathews. The two brothers are called Polyneices and Peteocles, the latter name with its initial 'P' stressing the fact that they are essentially similar. Peteocles is 'The Salvator mundi ... the strongarm, the singlehanded', the man who has saved the city. But Antigone champions her other brother Polyneices not by burying him, but by inscribing the initial of his name on every wall left standing: 'P'. Equally well, Antigone's assertion that she represents 'tens of thousands of faceless women. Women who stand in queues, and wait. And their waiting is more busy, more concentrated, than all the bustle of men'[45] reflects not merely the man/woman clash in Sophocles, but also the sociological fact that women in fifth century Athens and in modern Ireland lack the sort of power enjoyed by men.

8

Brendan Kennelly's version of *Antigone*, which is written in stanzas of short lines with effective repetition and some rhyme, departs from Sophocles in a number of ways: it omits much of the cultural material that is specifically Greek in favour of what is abstract and universal; it rewrites some of the Choral Odes; and it reduces the chorus to a single man. But what most distinguishes Kennelly's *Antigone* is his privileging of the male/female conflict in the play, that between Creon and Antigone. Kennelly is, of course, aware of the fact that this conflict relates to the burial of Polyneices: 'Antigone is in the grip of her vision of justice and she wants to make it reality. Creon, too, is in the grip of his vision and he is determined to make it prevail. But Antigone's vision of justice, love and loyalty is not Creon's'.[46] In the face of the implacable male ruler (who owes something to Kennelly's portrayal of Cromwell) – 'I am determined Creon' – Antigone is equally uncompromising: 'Polyneices is my brother./I can't be false to him'.[47]

Nevertheless, what Kennelly stresses is the clash between a young woman in revolt and an older man with authority. When mapped onto contemporary Ireland, this revolt of the other subtly suggests an attack on a calcified patriarchy by feminists and liberals, who seek less rigid attitudes to issues of gender and of sexuality.

In Kennelly, Creon and Antigone classify each other in terms of gender as 'girl' and 'man', but Creon is unwilling to accommodate the resulting concept of *difference*. Antigone, who is 'wild', says to him, 'You fear the thoughts of difference', and Haemon vainly tells him to listen to 'different voices'. But Creon stresses his innate superiority as a man – 'I would be no man,/She would be the man/If I let her go unpunished'; he attacks Haemon for suggesting the opposite – 'You would put a man below a woman' – and so tells him to 'be a woman'. Here the worlds of men and women are mutually incomprehensible, as Antigone asks, 'What man/Knows anything of women?' And yet if Antigone was saved from dying in a hole among the rocks, 'I could change all the men of the world'.

One thing that seems to link Creon and Antigone is language, the noun 'word' being constantly reiterated in the play. The Chorus tell Creon: 'You have the power to turn your word to action'; Antigone says, 'Word and deed are one in me'. But the two situations are in reality wholly dissimilar: Creon's word leads to injustice; Antigone's word to justice.[48]

There are further resonances that turn Kennelly's *Antigone* into 'a feminist declaration of independence'.[49] Kennelly well understands the vital importance to Antigone of being a sister, which leads to her notorious assertion that she would rather bury a brother than a husband or a child:

> In *Antigone* ... I wanted to explore sisterhood, the loyalty a sister will show to a brother, against law, against marriage, against everything. There's no relationship like it; it has all the passion of your whole nature, this side of incest ... it was a study of a girl whose impulses defied everything, in order to bury the boy, to give him dignity.[50]

Hence Antigone's statement:[51]

> A lost child can be replaced
> And other husbands can be found.
> But when my father and mother are dead
> No brother's life
> Can ever flower in me again.
> In me flourished the very best of men.

Kennelly is also more explicit than Sophocles in positing romantic love between Antigone and Haemon: Antigone cries (it is Ismene in Sophocles) 'Haemon, Haemon, my beloved', and Ismene states: 'But never again can there be such love/As bound these two together./Their two hearts are one./If Antigone dies, so does your son'. Finally, the matter of Eurydice. In Sophocles, Eurydice speaks only nine lines, but in Kennelly she speaks thirty, so that her anguish at the death of her son Haemon becomes more vivid. Once more it is the experience of women that counts.

---

[1] B.M.W. Knox, *The Heroic Temper* (Berkeley/Los Angeles: University of California Press, 1966), pp. 62-116; D.A. Hester, *Mnemosyne* 24(1971), pp. 11-59; G. Steiner, *Antigones* (Oxford: Oxford University Press, 1984); H.P. Foley in *Tragedy and the Tragic*, ed. M.S. Silk (Oxford: Oxford University Press, 1996), pp. 49-73; M. Trapp, *ibid.*, pp. 74-84; D. Franklin and J. Harrison, *Sophocles – Antigone* (Cambridge: Cambridge University Press, 2003); M. Griffith, *Sophocles – Antigone* (Cambridge: Cambridge University Press, 2003).

[2] F. Macintosh, *Dying Acts* (Cork: Cork University Press, 1994), pp. 19-38, esp. pp. 19-21.

[3] N. Loraux, *Tragic Ways of Killing a Woman* (Cambridge, Mass.: Yale University Press), 1987.

[4] M. Shaw, *Classical Philology* 70(1975), pp. 255-66.

[5] Steiner (note 1).

[6] F. Macintosh in *The Cambridge Companion to Greek Tragedy*, ed. P.E. Easterling (Cambridge: Cambridge University Press, 1997), pp. 285-88.

[7] Matthew Arnold, Preface to *Poems* (1983).

[8] Tom Paulin, *The Riot Act* (London: Faber & Faber, 1985); Aidan Mathews, Antigone, Unpublished Ms. 1984 (I am grateful to Mr. Mathews for making his play available to me); Brendan Kennelly, *Antigone* (Newcastle-upon-Tyne: Bloodaxe, 1996); Conall Morrison, *Antigone* Unpublished Ms. 2003 (I am grateful to Ms. N. Remoundou for making this play available to me); Seamus Heaney, *The Burial at Thebes* (London: Faber & Faber, 2004). For comment on Paulin, Mathews and Kennelly see A. Roche in *Cultural Contexts and Literary Idioms in Contemporary Irish Literature*, ed. M. Kennelly (Gerrards Cross: Colin Smythe, 1988), pp. 221-50; C. Murray in *Perspectives of Irish Drama and Theatre*, eds. J. Genet and R. Cave (Gerrards Cross: Colin Smythe, 1991), pp. 115-29. For Kennelly see also D. Cairns, *Classics Ireland* 5(1988), pp. 14-46; K. McCracken in *Dark Fathers into Light: Brendan Kennelly*, ed. R. Pine (Newcastle-upon-Tyne: Bloodaxe, 1994), pp. 114-47 (also dealing with *Medea* and *The Trojan Women*).

[9] C.P. Segal in *Sophocles*, ed. T. Woodard (Englewood Cliffs, N.J.: Prentice-Hall, 1966), pp. 62-85; Martin Heidegger, *ibid.*, pp. 86-90.

[10] D. Franklin and J. Harrison, *Sophocles – Antigone* (Cambridge: Cambridge University Press, 2003), p. 27.

[11] Cf. the standard Greek-English dictionary, Liddle, Scott, Jones, s.v. *deinos*; also A. Poole, *Tragedy* (Oxford: Oxford University Press, 2005), p. 27: 'No single English word will do justice to the power of the Greek epithet *deinos* – wonderful, terrible, awesome, sacred'.

[12] H. Lloyd-Jones, *Sophocles – Antigone, The Women of Trachis, Philoctetes, Oedipus at Colonus* (Cambridge, Mass/London: Harvard University Press, 2002), p. 35; A.H. Sommerstein, *Greek Drama and Dramatists* (London/New York: Routledge, 2002), p. 102.

[13] D. Grene and R. Lattimore, *Antigone* (New York: University of Chicago Press, 1970), p. 87; R. Fagles, *Sophocles – The Three Theban Plays* (Harmondsworth: Penguin, 1984), p. 76.

[14] Paulin (note 8), p. 23; Kennelly (note 8), p. 18; Morrison (note 8); Heaney (note 8), p. 16.

[15] For comment on O'Brien see Tom Paulin, *Ireland and the English Crisis* (Newcastle-upon-Tyne: Bloodaxe, 1987), pp. 25-31; Steiner (note 1), pp. 190-91.

[16] O'Brien quoted in Paulin (note 8), p. 26.

[17] Lloyd-Jones, quoted *ibid.*, p. 28.

[18] Paulin (note 8), p. 18; p. 15; p. 23.

[19] *ibid.*, p. 15.

[20] *ibid.*, p. 11.

[21] *ibid.*, p. 13.

[22] B. Hardy in *Yeats, Sligo and Ireland*, ed. A.N. Jeffares (Gerrards Cross: Colin Smythe, 1980), pp. 31-55.

[23] Paulin (note 8), p. 60; p. 61; p. 58.

[24] Roche (note 8), p. 229.

[25] Paulin (note 8), p. 12.

[26] *ibid.*, p. 23; p. 44.

[27] There are no page numbers in the typescript of Morrison's *Antigone*.

[28] Seamus Heaney, *The Sunday Times*, March 21, 2004.

[29] *ibid.*

[30] Heaney (note 8), pp. 14-15.

[31] *ibid.*, pp. 16-17.

[32] Fagles (note 13), p. 77.

[33] Heaney (note 28).

[34] Heaney (note 8), p. 3; p. 6.

[35] *ibid.*, p. 10.

[36] *ibid.*, p. 12.

[37] *ibid.*, p. 17; p. 22.

[38] Cf. e.g., J. McFarlane in *Modernism*, eds. M. Bradbury and J. McFarlane (Harmondsworth: Penguin, 1985), pp. 561-70.

[39] Mathews (note 8), p. 27; p. 10; p. 12; p. 36; p. 10; p. 52; p. 64.

[40] *ibid.*, p. 36; p. 56.

[41] R. Girard, *Violence and the Sacred* (Baltimore 1977).

[42] Mathews (note 8), p. 51.

[43] Quotations from Murray (note 8), p. 128.

[44] Mathews (note 8), p. 1; p. 54.

[45] *ibid.*, p. 19; p. 36.

[46] Kennelly in Kennelly (note 8), p. 50.

[47] Kennelly (note 8), p. 27; p. 9.

[48] *ibid.*, p. 21; p. 7; p. 24; p. 30; p. 22; p. 32; p. 35.

[49] Kennelly, quoted in Roche (note 8), p. 242.

[50] Kennelly, quoted in McCracken (note 8), p. 124.

[51] Kennelly (note 8), p. 37.

4 | Sophocles' *King Oedipus* and *Oedipus at Colonus*

1

Already viewed by Aristotle as the paradigm of Athenian tragedy and adumbrating the genre of the detective story in a very brief way (1530 lines), *King Oedipus* is (after Antigone) Sophocles' most famous play.[1] Here classic technique is used to deal with a highly dysfunctional, highly deviant family. In psychological terms, the family exhibits over-valuation of love objects when Oedipus marries his mother Jocasta, and when his daughter Antigone dies for her brother Polyneices; it exhibits under-valuation of love objects when Oedipus kills his father Laius, and when the brothers Polyneices and Eteocles kill each other. Such a grotesque family demonstrate how the city of Thebes can be staged as the Other of Athens.[2]

In Sophocles, the myth of Oedipus runs as follows.[3] When a son Oedipus is born to the king and queen of Thebes, Laius and Jocasta, the Delphic Oracle, the chief religious authority of the Greek world, prophesies that he will kill his father and marry his mother. To frustrate the oracle, Laius and Jocasta decide to expose the boy on Mount Cithaeron with his foot transfixed by a spike, so that he may die of neglect. But a Theban shepherd rescues Oedipus, and hands him over to a Corinthian shepherd, who brings him to Corinth; there he is raised as their own child by the king and queen, Polybus and Merope. Later, when Oedipus learns of the oracle about himself, he flees Corinth to frustrate it (as he thinks). At a place where three roads meet, Oedipus quarrels with an older man and kills him; this is his father Laius. When Oedipus comes to Thebes, he solves the riddle of the Sphinx, ridding the city of that monster and marrying the queen; this is his mother Jocasta. Some years after these events,

Sophocles' tragedy *King Oedipus* begins: a plague has descended because of Laius' unsolved murder (this may suggest the plague in Athens in 430 BC) and Oedipus, as king, must find out who did it.

A crucial aspect of Sophocles' handling of the Oedipus myth is that he omits any reference to a curse on the house of Laius that arose out of his homosexual seduction of a boy named Chrysippus.[4] This means that the horrific events that befall Oedipus have no obvious rationale, but are wholly arbitrary. The gods exist, intervene in human affairs, are inscrutable. We cannot know *why* these things happen to Oedipus; all we know is that they do.

Nevertheless, there is in *King Oedipus* a great stress on the theme of knowledge, with Oedipus a symbol of human intelligence who resolutely pursues the truth. Indeed the name Oedipus (Greek Oidipous) connotes not just 'swollen foot' (a reference to the spike), but also 'I know where'.[5] As Oedipus investigates Laius' murder, he exemplifies the procedures of the Athenian legal system and the cleverness of the Sophistic movement. More: Oedipus suggests the Athenian leader Pericles, a powerful, vigorous, intelligent ruler who mirrors the role of Athens as a democracy that is also a tyranny.[6]

But for all of Oedipus' knowledge and power, he is, at the end of the day, a radically dual person[7] – as the prophet Tiresias points out (lines 447-62). Consider the following: Oedipus is the Corinthian who is Theban, king and beggar, doctor and disease, detective and criminal, saviour of the city and its scapegoat, the solver of riddles who can't solve his own, sighted without insight and blind with insight, son and killer of Laius, son and husband of Jocasta, brother and father of his four children. Thus Oedipus is the paradigmatic example in Western theatre of a person who is dual, and it is this radical duality and not the so-called Oedipus complex that makes him the archetypal character.[8] The most telling argument against the Oedipus complex is that Oedipus, as an adult, explicitly set out to *avoid* killing his father and marrying his mother. And when he does commit parricide and incest, he is wholly unaware of this.

Sophocles' tragedy appears to end in disaster: Jocasta hangs herself; Oedipus blinds himself, which is a punishment for sexual sin,[9] and he loses the throne (as he does not in Homer's *Odyssey*); the blackness is stressed by the final pessimism of the Chorus.[10] But at the same time, Oedipus emerges as a man who faces up, without flinching and with great energy, to his appalling situation: he defends his decision to blind himself, he demands to be sent into exile, he refers to the fact that he enjoys a special destiny.[11] As Knox says, *King Oedipus* 'presents us with a terrible affirmation of man's subordinate position in the universe, and at the same time with a heroic vision of man's victory in defeat'.[12]

2

Irish appropriation of Sophocles' *King Oedipus* takes the form of versions by Yeats and by Mary Elizabeth Burke-Kennedy, and a loose adaptation by Synge.

Sophocles was attractive to Yeats because he could be enlisted to meet Yeats's theatrical requirements at a given time. Initially, when Yeats wanted Irish dramas to possess elemental or folk characteristics based on an extravagant imagination and to play to an unsophisticated audience, Sophocles' mythical characters could be regarded as possessing that type of imagination, and his motley Athenian audience compared to that which listened to Irish-speaking story-tellers in Irish cabins. Later, when Yeats became preoccupied with the anti-realistic and aristocratic Noh drama of Japan, Sophocles served as exemplar of a non-naturalistic theatre fully intelligible only to an intellectual elite.

Yeats is very emphatic about why he chose to translate *King Oedipus*: he follows Aristotle in regarding it as 'the greatest masterpiece of Greek drama', and he records its profound, religious impact upon him: 'In rehearsal I had but one overwhelming emotion, a sense of the actual presence in a terrible sacrament of the god. But I have got that always, though never before so strongly, from Greek drama'.[13]

Yeats preserves the invariant core of Sophocles' play;[14] the relentless search for the truth by Oedipus, and the king's radical duality that mirrors Yeats's own obsession with opposites. But Yeats makes a major change towards the end of *King Oedipus*: he omits 82 of the last 234 lines, so that he abbreviates drastically the self-pity of the blind, parricidal and incestuous king and heavily stresses instead the energy of Oedipus. Hence Yeats's Oedipus exhibits a heroism that is close to his emphasis on the swordsman and Homeric-type courage; for self-pity of any kind is anathema to his unchristened heart.

Yeats is very free in his treatment of the Choral Odes, which read like variations on a theme by Sophocles. As a result, when the Greek director Cacoyannis directed Yeats's *King Oedipus* for the Abbey in 1973, he enlisted the poet Richard Murphy – who held that Yeats wrote beautiful lyrical choruses which killed the drama in Sophocles

– to restore the original material.[15] In some of the Choral Odes, Yeats again stresses the theme of heroism: in the Second and Third Choral Odes, he emphasizes first the heroic nature of man, and second the mental and physical abilities of Oedipus. In contrast, in the Fourth Choral Ode, Yeats stresses Oedipus' horrible position as son and husband of Jocasta.

Yeats's diction in *King Oedipus* is (as he said of the Messenger speech) 'bare, hard and natural as a saga'. Aiming to turn Jebb's 'half Latin, half Victorian dignity' that involves archaisms into 'speakable English', he and Lady Gregory 'went through it all, altering every sentence that might not be intelligible on the Blasket Islands'.[16] The result can be judged from this section of the Messenger's speech about the suicide of Jocasta and Oedipus' self-blinding:[17]

> There we saw the woman hanging in a swinging halter, and with a terrible cry he loosened the halter from her neck. When that unhappiest woman lay stretched upon the ground, we saw another dreadful sight. He dragged the golden brooches from her dress and lifting them struck them upon his eyeballs, crying out, 'You have looked enough upon those you ought never to have looked upon, failed long enough to know those that you should have known, henceforth you shall be dark'. He struck his eyes, not once, but many times, lifting his hands and speaking such or like words. The blood poured down and out with a few slow drops, but all at once over his beard in a dark shower as it were hail.

Yeats's *King Oedipus* has had a number of important productions. His concept of Oedipus as an isolated heroic figure was stressed in the London production of 1945, directed by Michel Saint-Denis and with Lawrence Olivier as Oedipus, and by the Stratford, Ontario production of 1955, directed by Tyrone Guthrie and with Douglas Campbell as Oedipus.[18]

The production of Yeats's *King Oedipus* by the Druid Theatre Company in Galway in 1987, directed by Garry Hynes, was marked by two striking innovations: Oedipus was played by a woman, Marie Mullen (reversing Greek practice in which men played women), and the Chorus consisted of a single actor, Michael Forde.[19]

Edward (Lord) Longford wrote a translation of *King Oedipus* that was put on in the Gate Theatre in 1942. Anew McMaster's inspired playing of Oedipus was described by Christopher Casson (who played Tiresias) as 'one of those exquisite moments of theatre to be remembered all one's life'.[20]

3

Irish appropriations of Sophocles continued into the new millennium, when in 2000 Mary Elizabeth Burke-Kennedy wrote a play called *Oedipus*,[21] 'a new version of the myth' that preserves the invariant core of *King Oedipus*, but makes technical and thematic changes. A radical technical innovation is to divide the Chorus into nine parts, so as to provide a running commentary by a series of individual people on what is happening, and to bring out more fully for the audience the precise import of events; to stress, for example, the political resistance in Thebes to investigating the murder of Laius.

New material inserted by Burke-Kennedy comes in a Prologue about Oedipus solving the Riddle of the Sphinx, in a scene set in Corinth with Oedipus' adoptive parents, and in a scene set in the bedroom of Oedipus and Jocasta after they learn the truth. By making more explicit those parts of the story, these scenes serve to humanize Oedipus and to make his eventual fate even more appalling. Burke-Kennedy's lengthy Prologue (which involves the use of the divided Chorus) chronicles in considerable detail the devastation in Thebes brought about by the Sphinx; the riddles that the Sphinx puts to Oedipus and his correct answers; the happy marriage of Oedipus and Jocasta; and the plague that has (after twelve years) caused destruction and death in Thebes. In the scene set in Corinth with Oedipus' adoptive parents king Polybus and queen Merope, celebrations are held in honour of Oedipus' birthday. Polybus' nephew Telaman questions Oedipus' parentage, and sets in train the inexorable sequence of events that lead to Oedipus' downfall.

The bedroom scene between Oedipus and Jocasta that takes place after the truth about Oedipus becomes known renders the situation both more poignant and more awful:[22]

> JOCASTA: Like husband, like wife.
> OEDIPUS: Those names can never more be used.
> JOCASTA: That is what we are. Incestuous.
> OEDIPUS: Innocent in the committing of that crime.
> JOCASTA: Only while ignorant of who we were.
> OEDIPUS: Until this very night – an hour or so ago.
> JOCASTA: But in that hour or so, and in full knowledge
> I have continued to love Oedipus,
> My husband.
> OEDIPUS: Don't say that.

JOCASTA: No more lies. I now know who you are.
I love you.

Burke-Kennedy writes *Oedipus* in a succinct, vigorous register of language, as Teiresias' indictment of Oedipus' duality shows:[23]

> You demand to know the killers of Laius.
> It is just one man. He is here.
> A Theban born and bred.
> He came here with sight – he will leave blind.
> He is rich now – he will leave destitute to live forever in exile.
> He is loved now. He will be a pariah.
> The syphilitic and the leper will be embraced before him.
> The husband of his mother;
> the brother of his children;
> the killer and supplanter of his father.
> Look in the glass and find him.

4

The content of this and the previous chapter would be somewhat different if the play originally due to be staged at the Abbey Theatre on January 29, 1907 had gone ahead: that play was a translation of Sophocles' *Antigone* by Robert Gregory (who read Classics at New College, Oxford). But instead of what could now be seen as yet another Irish appropriation of *Antigone*, the audience were treated to Synge's masterpiece *The Playboy of the Western World*, which appeared to be a wholly Irish play. But Synge, who knew Greek and had already written a tragedy called *Riders to the Sea* that exhibited Greek qualities[24] (Aeschylus and Sophocles combined, according to Yeats!),[25] now produced in *The Playboy* a comedy that was, *inter alia*, an inversion of Sophocles' *King Oedipus*.[26] As Grene says, '*The Playboy* is a comedy and it plays comic games with the tragic legend of Oedipus: Christy does *not* succeed in killing his father, he does *not* marry either of the available mother-substitutes'[27] (Pegeen Mike and the Widow Quin). The reason that the character of Oedipus can so readily be mapped onto Christy Mahon is that person's plasticity, his ability to assume any shape.[28]

Oedipus kills his father, and, when the truth of this emerges, he is scorned and abandoned. Christy does not kill his father, but pretends he has, and, because of this deed, is treated like a hero, discovering powers he never thought he had and winning all before him in the athletic competition; this is his form of self-recognition (*anagnorisis*). Christy is installed as pot-boy in the pub owned by Michael James Flatherty, and becomes an object of erotic interest to Pegeen Mike, the publican's daughter, and to the Widow Quin. This widow is indeed a Jocasta-figure, who is maternally erotic in the first half of the play and maternally protective in the second,[29] while Pegeen Mike proposes to marry Christy; hence his reference to 'two fine women fighting for the likes of me'.[30]

The reversal (*peripeteia*) of Synge's play is the polar opposite of that in *King Oedipus*: Christy has *not* killed his father, who, in comic fashion, appears on stage. The ending of *The Playboy* is also partly comic because Christy has turned into a successful person: while he does not remain with either Pegeen Mike or the Widow Quin (as a conventional comedy would require), Christy has gained immense strength from his experiences in Mayo, aiming to control his father in future and asserting that 'I'm master of all fights from now'.[31] As Oedipus clearly was not.

5

Written not long before his death in 406 BC, and produced in 401 BC by his grandson, Sophocles' play *Oedipus at Colonus*[32] deals with the final stages of the myth of Oedipus. Oedipus has been banished from Thebes by Creon, while his two sons Eteocles and Polyneices do nothing to help him. Accompanied by his daughter Antigone, Oedipus – old, blind, ragged, suppliant – has arrived at the sacred grove of the Eumenides in Colonus, an area of Attica north of Athens (it was Sophocles' birthplace). The local inhabitants wish Oedipus to leave, but he is determined to stay because he has learnt from an oracle of Apollo that Colonus is the place in which he will die. It is indeed the case that Oedipus' will and strong moral sense becomes paramount in the play, but here involves no hint of self-destruction (contrast Antigone and Philoctetes). Theseus, king of Athens, a model ruler, who represents the city at its finest, promises to look after Oedipus, and to afford him burial in Attica, so that his spirit will protect Athens. Hence the myth of Oedipus is transferred from the city of his birth Thebes to the city of the play's performance Athens, and this transfer suggests the historical hostility between Thebes and Athens (not least at the time *Oedipus at Colonus* was written towards the end of the Peloponnesian War).[33] Indeed Sophocles provides an eloquent panegyric of Athens as a model city in the First Choral Ode (668-719), a valedictory celebration of its greatness before the final defeat by Sparta in 404 BC

Oedipus must, however, contend with the appearance of Creon and of Polyneices. Creon, who is quite unscrupulous, wants Thebes to possess Oedipus' body, so it can enjoy the power it brings, but will locate Oedipus only on the borders of Theban territory because of the pollution his parricide and incest have incurred (crimes heavily stressed in the play). Creon's guards seize Antigone and Ismene whose account of the quarrel between her brothers Eteocles and Polyneices for the throne of Thebes has angered Oedipus; Creon himself is about to lay hands on Oedipus, when Theseus intervenes, and rescues him and his daughters. When Polyneices arrives, he is repentant about the way he treated Oedipus, but wants his help in his contest with Eteocles. Oedipus refuses and savagely, in superhuman anger, curses both his sons. In the face of human greed for power, Oedipus, once a ruler, is resolute in refusing to play that game.

When peals of thunder indicate that Oedipus' death is imminent, he withdraws to a lonely place and dies there. This death is, in some way, supernatural, and, although Theseus witnesses it, he will tell only his heir what exactly occurred. Despite the mystery surrounding Oedipus' death, it is clear that he becomes a *hero*, a hugely powerful figure who, in return for the offering of sacrifice and cult, will protect the locality of Colonus in the future.[34] In spite of his awful crimes, Oedipus therefore enjoys a very special destiny, his mortal fragility transmuted into a transcendent state. The essentially tragic vision of *King Oedipus* gives way in *Oedipus at Colonus* to something much more positive: Oedipus is reintegrated into the city-state, the *polis*, as a citizen. And that *polis* is Athens.

6

Yeats moved on quickly from his version of *King Oedipus* – a 'great success'[35] at the Abbey in 1926 – to his version of *Oedipus at Colonus*,[36] which was staged at the Abbey in 1927. Yeats preserves the invariant core of Sophocles' play, and was specially keen on the grove of the Eumenides (Furies), and on Oedipus' supernatural death. So Yeats feels that the grove in Sophocles has Irish analogues: 'When I prepared *Oedipus at Colonus* for the Abbey stage I saw that the wood of the Furies in the opening scene was any Irish haunted wood'; 'when Oedipus at Colonus went into the wood of the Furies he felt the same creeping in his flesh that an Irish countryman feels in certain haunted woods in Galway and in Sligo'.[37]

For Yeats, Oedipus' special death makes him a central figure in mythology, in contrast to Christ who ascended into Heaven, and to the abstract philosophy of Plato:

Oedipus lay upon the earth at the middle point between four sacred objects, was there washed as the dead are washed, and thereupon passed with Theseus to the wood's heart until amidst the sound of thunder earth opened, 'riven by love', and he sank down soul and body into the earth.[38]

In his version of *Oedipus at Colonus*, Yeats places much more emphasis than Sophocles on Oedipus' supernatural death by cutting out entirely Antigone's laments at the death of her father and at her own plight. Once more Yeats's concept of Oedipus' heroism demands that anything which limits it be omitted, and through his miraculous death Oedipus finally bridges that crucial Yeatsian antinomy of swordsman and saint. Hence Yeats ends his play – as Sophocles does not – with the emphatic summation: 'God's will has been accomplished'.[39]

In writing *Oedipus at Colonus*, Yeats stated that 'I want to be less literal and more idiomatic and modern'.[40] In fact, Yeats turned Jebb into concise, hard-hitting, clear English that suggests Homer turned into prose. A fine example is the speech Oedipus makes following Ismene's revelation of his sons' refusal to accept him back into the city of Thebes (421-60):[41]

> Then may no god turn them from this war, may spear meet spear till I blast them from the tomb! I shall permit neither the son that now holds the throne to keep his throne, nor the son that is banished to return. They neither raised up their hands nor their voices to defend me driven out to shame and wandering. Say if you will that when the city drove me out it did the very thing I asked of it. No, I say, no! Upon that first day, when my soul was all in tumult and the dearest wish of my heart was to die, though I be stoned to death, no man would grant me my desire; but later on, when a long time had passed, when the tumult in my soul had passed, when I began to feel that in my anger against myself I had asked for punishments beyond my deserts, the city drove me out. My son, who might have hindered, did nothing, though one word could have changed everything, and I their father was driven out to wander through my life as a beggar and an outcast. I owe my daily bread and whatever I have found of care and shelter to my daughters, to these two girls. Their brothers have preferred the mob's favour; yes, they have trafficked with it and bartered away their father for throne and sceptre. Never, never shall Oedipus be ally of one or the other, never shall the throne of Thebes be lucky to one or the other. I meditate upon the new prophecies the girl has brought, and when I speak, Phoebus Apollo speaks. Nor shall I help the men of Thebes whether it be Creon that they send or any other that may be great amongst them. But, strangers, if you are

willing to help, if these Dreadful Goddesses are willing, I shall deliver your country from all its enemies.

As with *King Oedipus*, Yeats's treatment of the Choral Odes in *Oedipus at Colonus* verges on free composition. Yeats entitled his radically new version of the first Choral Ode 'Colonus' Praise',[42] and placed it, as a separate poem in the volume *The Tower*. Here Yeats asserts that his beloved concept of Unity of Being is located in Plato's Academy to the west of the city of Athens and near the river Cephisus. What thrives in the Academy is nothing less than a Platonic Form upon earth that has provided us with the seminal achievements of Athenian civilization: 'The self-sown, self-begotten shape that gives/Athenian intellect its mastery'. Equally well, a visitor to Colonus will find, in an emphatic phrase of approbation not appearing in Sophocles, 'the loveliest spectacle there is'.[43] Matching Athenian intellect is the most beautiful landscape in the world.

Sophocles' third Choral Ode deals in a pessimistic way with the basic problem of human life, suggesting that the best thing is never to be born, and the second best is to die as quickly as possible. Yeats replicates the first of these propositions, but subverts the pessimism of the second by opting for a cheery farewell:[44]

> Never to have lived is best, ancient writers say;
> Never to have drawn the breath of life, never to have
> looked into the eye of day;
> The second best's a gay goodnight and quickly turn away.

As Yeats wrote: 'the best line is very bad Grecian but very good Elizabethan and so it must stay'.[45]

7

Oxford University Press is publishing a series of new translations of Greek tragedies in the form of a collaboration between a poet and a classicist that include a substantial Introduction by the latter. So the Irish poet Eamon Grennan and the American classicist Rachel Kitzinger have produced a new translation of *Oedipus at Colonus*, with an Introduction by Kitzinger and a Translator's Note by Grennan.[46] It is noteworthy that this translation constitutes one of the very few *straight* translations of a Greek tragedy by an Irish author, giving us Sophocles without addition and subtraction (unlike Yeats), and so requiring us to consider what *Oedipus at Colonus* might have meant when it was first put on in Athens. So Grennan and Kitzinger require us to consider the strange story of

Oedipus in his final phase at Colonus; his moral authority in refusing to be used by the unscrupulous Creon and by the self-serving Polyneices; his miraculous death that will see him transformed into a powerful *hero*. Then Grennan and Kitzinger, unlike Yeats, preserve Antigone's laments at the death of her father, and so ensure a more balanced approach to that remarkable end.

The aim of Grennan and Kitzinger in their translation of *Oedipus at Colonus* is to provide 'a readable and, more important, a speakable text' in English that is 'without either antiquarian effects ... or too contemporary, colloquial a feel', but instead has 'the capacity to be plain, blunt, passionate, and lyrical by turns'. For the Choral Odes or exchanges with the Chorus, Grennan aims at 'a more pronounced lyrical feel and rhythmic presence' by enhancing 'the sense of the rhythmic unit of the *line* (as opposed to the sentence).[47]

Two examples, one from the Episodes and one from the Choral Odes, will serve to illustrate the success of Grennan and Kitzinger in their translation. Here is Oedipus castigating his sons Eteocles and Polyneices, and praising his daughters Antigone and Ismene:[48]

> Ach, those two! In their nature, in their way of life,
> they mimic Egyptian habits. For the men of Egypt
> sit indoors weaving, while their wives
> go out every day in the world
> to provide what they need. So here you both are,
> while those fit for the task do housework
> like maids. The two of you do their work, this hard work –
> caring for my suffering self. This girl here,
> since she grew from a child into a woman's strong body
> has tramped through misfortune, leading an old man.
> Often barefoot, often hungry,
> she's crossed wild woodland, and often
> under scorching sun or drenching rain
> she's toiled in patience, not giving a thought
> to home or comfort or food for herself –
> so long as her father has enough to eat.

Grennan and Kitzinger capture in an emphatic way (without Elizabethan commentary) the famous pessimism of the third Choral Ode in *Oedipus at Colonus*, which is an integral part of the Greek view of life:[49]

> Never to be born is the best story.
> But when one can come to the light of day
> second-best is to leave and go back
> quick as you can back where you came from.
> For in his giddy light-headed youth

what sharp blow isn't far from a man? What affliction –
strife death dissension the ache of envy –
isn't close by? And in the end
his lot is to lack all power:
despised and cast out in friendless old age
where a man lives with nothing
but one hardship topping another.

---

[1] For editions of *King Oedipus* see R. Jebb, *Sophocles: Oedipus Tyranus* (Cambridge: Cambridge University Press, 1890); R.D. Dawe, ed., *Sophocles – Oedipus Rex* (Cambridge: Cambridge University Press, 1982); for comment see B. Knox, *Oedipus at Thebes* (New Haven/London: Yale University Press, 1998).

[2] F.I. Zeitlin in *Nothing to do with Dionysus: Athenian Drama in its Social Context*, eds. J.J. Winkler and F. Zeitlin (Princeton: Princeton University Press, 1990), pp. 130-67.

[3] L. Edmunds, *Oedipus – The Ancient Legend and its Later Analogues* (Baltimore/London: The Johns Hopkins University Press, 1996).

[4] Euripides, *Phoenician Women* 1608-11.

[5] S. Goldhill, *Arethusa*.

[6] Knox (note 1), pp. 53-106.

[7] J.-P. Vernant in J.-P. Vernant and P. Vidal-Naquet, *Myth and Tragedy in Ancient Greece* (New York: Zone Books, 1990), pp. 113-40.

[8] J.-P. Vernant in Vernant and Vidal-Naquet (note 7), pp. 85-111.

[9] G. Devereux, *Journal of Hellenic Studies* 93(1973), pp. 36-49.

[10] B. Arkins, *Classical Quarterly* 38(1988), pp. 555-58.

[11] Knox (note 1), 185-96; G. Gellie, *Ramus* 15(1986), pp. 35-42.

[12] Knox (note 1), p. 196.

[13] Letter of 15 August, 1909, quoted by D.R. Clark and J.B. McGuire, *Yeats – Annual of Critical and Textual Studies* 2(1984), 47; *The Letters of W.B. Yeats*, ed. A. Wade (London: Rupert Hart-Davis, 1950), p. 720.

[14] F.D. Grab, *Journal of English and Germanic Literature* 71(1972), pp. 336-54; B. Arkins, *Builders of My Soul: Greek and Roman Themes in Yeats* (Gerrards Cross: Colin Smythe, 1990), pp. 124-41; P.Th.R.G. Liebregts, *Centaurs in the Twilight – W.B. Yeats's Use of the Classical Tradition* (Amsterdam/Atlanta: Rodopi, 1993), pp. 359-71.

[15] R. Schull, *The Arts in Ireland* 2(1973), pp. 15-21.

[16] Yeats, *Letters* (note 13), p. 720; p. 537.

[17] W.B. Yeats, *Collected Plays* (London: Macmillan, 1950), p. 512.

[18] F. Macintosh in *The Cambridge Companion to Greek Tragedy*, ed. P.E. Easterling (Cambridge: Cambridge University Press, 1997), pp. 309-11.

[19] B. Arkins, *Theatre Ireland* 14(1988), pp. 22-23 and *Révue de Littérature Comparée* 63(1989), pp. 85-86.

[20] J. Cowell, *No Prophet but the Name – The Longfords and the Gate Theatre* (Dublin: Macmillan 1988), p. 148.

[21] Mary Elizabeth Burke-Kennedy, *Oedipus* (2000); I am grateful to Ms. Burke-Kennedy for supplying me with a typescript of her play. For comment on her plays see A. McMullan in *Theatre Stuff: Critical*

Essays on Contemporary Irish Theatre (Dublin: Carysfort Press, 2000), pp. 36-39.
[22] Burke-Kennedy (note 21), pp. 60-61.
[23] *ibid.*, p. 30.
[24] D. Johnston, *John Millington Synge* (New York/London: Columbia University Press, 1965), pp. 18-23.
[25] Yeats, quoted in J.M. *Synge – Interviews and Recollections*, ed. E.H. Mikhail (London: Longman, 1977), p. 120.
[26] D.J. Conacher, *Phoenix* 23(1969), pp. 26-38.
[27] N. Grene, *The Politics of Irish Drama* (Cambridge: Cambridge University Press, 1999), p. 95.
[28] D. Kiberd, *Inventing Ireland* (London: Jonathan Cape, 1995), pp. 180-81.
[29] Conacher (note 26), p. 35.
[30] J.M. Synge, *Plays* (Oxford: Oxford University Press, 1969), p.125.
[31] *ibid.*, p. 163.
[32] For *Oedipus at Colonus* see B.M.W. Knox, *The Heroic Temper* (Berkeley/Los Angeles: University of California Press, 1966), pp. 143-62; C.H. Whitman in *Sophocles*, ed. T. Woodard (Englewood Cliffs, N.J.: Prentice-Hall, 1966), pp. 146-74; P. Vidal-Nacquet in Vernant and Vidal-Naquet (note 7), pp. 329-59.
[33] E. Hall in Easterling (note 18), pp. 102-03.
[34] Whitman (note 32), pp. 130-51.
[35] Yeats (note 13), p. 720.
[36] Arkins and Liebregts (note 14).
[37] W.B. Yeats, *Explorations* (London: Macmillan, 1962), p. 438.
[38] W.B. Yeats, *A Vision* (London: Macmillan, 1937), p. 27.
[39] Yeats (note 17), p. 575.
[40] Yeats (note 13), p. 721.
[41] Yeats (note 17), pp. 535-36.
[42] B. Arkins, *Classical and Modern Literature* 7(1986), pp. 39-42; Arkins (note 14), pp. 136-38.
[43] Yeats (note 17), p. 544.
[44] ibid., p. 561.
[45] Yeats (note 13), p. 723.
[46] Eamon Grennan and Rachel Kitzinger, *Sophocles – Oedipus at Colonus* (New York: Oxford University Press, 2005).
[47] *ibid.*, p. 30; p. 31.
[48] *ibid.*, p. 50.
[49] *ibid.*, p. 84.

5 | Sophocles' *Philoctetes*

Like so many surviving Greek tragedies and like more than one third of Sophocles' plays, Philoctetes, which was staged in Athens in 409 BC, and won first prize, relates to the Trojan War.[1] When the Greeks were on their way to Troy, Philoctetes was bitten on the feet by a snake, and, because his unhealed wound stank so much, the Greeks, persuaded by Odysseus, abandoned him on the deserted coast of the island of Lemnos. After many years the Trojan prophet Helenus revealed that Troy would not fall to the Greeks, unless Philoctetes was persuaded to fight with his invincible bow and arrows (originally belonging to Heracles). Sophocles' play Philoctetes deals with the efforts of Odysseus and Neoptolemus, son of Achilles, to persuade Philoctetes to come to Troy with them. The central clash of values in Philoctetes is between those of Philoctetes and of Odysseus. Outrageously wronged by the Greeks and by Odysseus in particular, living a lonely, painful existence for years because of them, Philoctetes exemplifies the isolation (literal and metaphorical) and the intransigence of the Sophoclean hero. Resolutely refusing to compromise because he was so wronged, Philoctetes sticks to his principles no matter what: 'Never. Never!' is an apt summary of his position.

Trying to wear down Philoctetes' lonely resistance is Odysseus, who owes something to the type of the Athenian demagogue, a consummate talker and moral relativist who clearly believes that the end justifies the means (he is already here the trickster of later tradition). Unique to Sophocles is the use by Odysseus of an intermediary, the young man Neoptolemus. This youth's fundamental value system is that of his father, Achilles. He is violent, yet honourable – but initially he is corrupted by Odysseus and deceives Philoctetes in order to get the bow (a powerful dramatic prop). Neoptolemus then repents of his deceit and reverts to Achilles' value system: he returns the bow to Philoctetes and, failing to persuade him to go to Troy, he decides to take him home to Greece (as he had promised earlier). This conversion of Neoptolemus anticipates Philoctetes yielding to Heracles.

The change in Neoptolemus relates to the initiation process in the Athenian institution of the *ephebeia*, in which a young man becomes an adult at the age of eighteen and undergoes military training[2]. Situated in a frontier zone, the ephebe represents loyalty and solidarity, as seen in the famous oath that pledges he will not bring shame on his weapons or abandon his companions. But the ephebe also represents cunning, as seen in his sacrifice of his hair during the festival of the Apatouria (held in October-November). Neoptolemus passes during the course of *Philoctetes* through the stages of the ephebe's initiation: first he uses the language of deceit to entrap Philoctetes, a tricky ephebe who steals Philoctetes from himself; he then overcomes his confusion (which may represent that of the typical viewer of an Athenian tragedy), returns to his original Achillean self, and proves loyal to his ephebic oath.

What makes Philoctetes different from other plays of Sophocles is that, since we know that the efforts to persuade Philoctetes will succeed – Troy, after all, fell – our attention is directed not only to the hero, but also to the methods used to influence him. There are indeed right and wrong methods – deceit, force, persuasion – and the right method must be found: two wrong methods, deceit and force, fail, as does the right method of persuasion, now fatally compromised by the earlier wrong methods.

To break the impasse caused by Philoctetes' continuing intransigence, we need a *deus ex machina*: Heracles appears from the dead and announces that Zeus' plan for Philoctetes is that he go to Troy. Philoctetes acquiesces, takes part in Troy's fall, is healed. This happy ending, taken with the ambiguous death of Oedipus in *Oedipus at Colonus*, shows that in his late plays of old age Sophocles was capable of a more benign view than that presented in earlier tragedies such as *King Oedipus* and *Antigone*.

2

Irish appropriation of Sophocles' *Philoctetes* takes the form of a straight translation by Desmond Egan (*Philoctetes*), a version by Seamus Heaney (*The Cure at Troy*), and a loose adaptation by

Sydney Smith (*Sherca*)3. The play had an earlier history in Ireland: in 1725, Thomas Sheridan (grandfather of Richard Brinsley) produced the first English translation of *Philoctetes*, and had it staged in Dublin before the Viceroy.

Desmond Egan's *Philoctetes*4 (the only one of these plays to preserve the original title) translates Sophocles' play into English directly from the Greek without addition or subtraction. Such fidelity to the original must be seen as paradoxically radical: Egan forces us to interrogate the source language play on its own terms, to examine what in Athens in 409 BC this play was about (as already outlined).

But Egan (in an essay on the Greeks) has also given the reasons he translated *Philoctetes*.5 For Egan, Sophocles produces 'that clear and steady gaze, that metaphysical honesty', which the best of Greek literature exemplifies; involving, in the case of *Philoctetes*, the exploration of 'some of the most profound issues touching on human life' in 'the simplest of plots'. This profundity is put before us in a mere 1471 lines that represent 'the ideal of conciseness'. And the appearance of Herakles as *deus ex machina* 'does not bring any instant resolution, nor alter the perspective' because 'the supernatural in Sophocles tends to shade into character-psychology and into theme'.

The success of Egan's language in Philoctetes refutes Virginia Woolf's dictum that 'It is useless to read Greek in translation: translators can but offer us a vague equivalent'.6 Egan represents the complex and startling language of Sophoclean dialogue and choral odes by means of an emphatic modern register of English, by hard, concrete language that is neither literal nor deviant, that avoids archaisms and neologisms, that is eminently speakable. Consider, for example, an early exchange between Odysseus and Neoptolemus:7

NEOPTOLEMUS: Well, what else do you want me to do then? Tell lies?
ODYSSEUS: I am ordering you to get the better of Philoctetes through cleverness.
NEOPTOLEMUS: But why must I take him by deceit and not by persuasion?
ODYSSEUS: There is no question of persuading – and you couldn't possibly capture him.
NEOPTOLEMUS: What terrible power has he that gives him confidence?

ODYSSEUS: Killer arrows that never miss!
NEOPTOLEMUS: Then isn't it dangerous to go near him at all?
ODYSSEUS: No – not if you trick him as I tell you.
NEOPTOLEMUS: But surely you agree that it's shameful to lie?
ODYSSEUS: Not if lying leads to survival!
NEOPTOLEMUS: How can anyone dare to say that?
ODYSSEUS: Listen, when you stand to gain something, you must not hesitate.
NEOPTOLEMUS: What advantage is it to me that he should come to Troy?
ODYSSEUS: Only that bow will capture Troy.
NEOPTOLEMUS: Am I not the one who will destroy it, as predicted?
ODYSSEUS: Neither you without the bow, nor it without you.
NEOPTOLEMUS: Well if that's the case, it must be tracked down.
ODYSSEUS: Remember, when you do this, you'll get two rewards.
NEOPTOLEMUS: What two? If I knew them, I would certainly not hesitate.
ODYSSEUS: You would be known as both clever and valiant.
NEOPTOLEMUS: All right! I'll put aside all shame and go through with it.

3

Heaney's play The Cure at Troy[8] also preserves the invariant core of Sophocles' *Philoctetes*, presenting the clash of values between Odysseus and Neoptolemus, and the obduracy of Philoctetes. For what Heaney finds in the play is 'a fascination with the conflict between the integrity of the personal bond and the exactions of the group's demand for loyalty', together with 'the pride in the wound that is stronger than the desire for a cure'.[9] But Heaney sometimes softens the extreme attitudes portrayed by Sophocles: in contrast to Sophocles, his Philoctetes does not curse Neoptolemus, and utters the very non-Sophoclean sentiment: 'Count your blessings and always be ready to pity other people'.[10]

Although Heaney's register of language involves some colloquial and Northern dialectal elements – 'Your slate is clean'; 'There's a mug .../Hagged out of a log' – it is as vigorously modern as Egan's, as in this early speech of Odysseus:[11]

> You are going to have to work out some way
> Of deceiving Philoctetes with a story.
> He'll ask you who you are and where you're from
> And you'll say Achilles' son, which will be true.
> And that you're on your voyage back from Troy,
> Heading home in a rage against the Greeks.

And you can make the rage look natural if you say
You were insulted.
You'll tell him
How the Greeks begged and coaxed you to join up
And leave your native place because you –
You and only you –
Were the man they absolutely needed.
Troy could not be taken without you.

The features that turn *The Cure at Troy* (first performed for the Field Day Theatre Company in Derry in 1990) into 'A Version' of *Philoctetes* clearly relate to the conflict between the unionist and the nationalist communities in Northern Ireland.

The title of Heaney's play suggests not only the healing of Philoctetes, but also the possible healing of Northern Ireland; as he said, 'I wanted the title to prefigure a benign and unexpected turn of events'.[12] Of even more contemporary relevance are the utterances of the Chorus that consists of three women, who might be regarded as mirroring the Women's Coalition in Northern Ireland (in *Philoctetes*, the only extant Athenian tragedy without a female character, they are men).

The opening statement of the Chorus in Heaney's play (for which there is no Sophoclean equivalent) views Odysseus, Neoptolemus and Herakles as intransigent people convinced they are right, as governed in such conviction by self-pity, and as locked into the repetition of past mistakes; at the same time, the Chorus itself and the audience are partly implicated in all of this. Equally well, Heaney sees the character of Philoctetes as 'an aspect of *every* intransigence, republican as well as Unionist'.[13]

In this grim scenario, it is art that must mediate between reality and what can be hoped for, just as Sophocles introduced Herakles as the *deus ex machina*: 'Poetry/allowed the god to speak'.[14] At the end of Heaney's play, the Chorus (who function for Herakles because Heaney 'simply had not the nerve to bring on a god two minutes from curtain')[15] produce further non-Sophoclean material about human suffering among both nationalist and unionist communities in Northern Ireland: 'A hunger-striker's father/Stands in the graveyard dumb./The police widow in veils/Faints at the funeral home'. Past experience therefore gives rise to the very Sophoclean sentiment 'Don't hope/On this side of the grave'. But just as Sophocles' hero Philoctetes is healed and a resolution is reached, so in Northern Ireland the 'miracle of self-healing' may come about 'On the far side of revenge', with the result that at last 'hope and history rhyme'. Then love becomes a validating, but precarious force: 'And the half-true rhyme is love'.[16]

4

Sydney Smith, who is a distinguished poet,[17] has produced a loose adaptation of Sophocles' *Philoctetes* in his play *Sherca*[18] which completely transfers the setting from ancient Greece to modern Ireland, with Lemnos in the North-east Aegean becoming Sherca off the west coast of Ireland (Smith lived for many years on the island of Inisbofin off the Galway coast). In *Sherca*, Smith makes fully explicit the political themes that are merely hinted at in Sophocles (and Egan), and only partially dealt with in Heaney. The politics concern the internal wranglings of a doctrinaire party in which, as Brendan Behan might say, the first item on the agenda is the split. The Philoctetes character, who is fittingly named Phil, has left the party, and now lives alone on the bleak, uninhabited island of Sherca. Two members of the party called O'Dea and Leo – who are the equivalents of Odysseus and Neoptolemus respectively – try to persuade Phil to rejoin the party. The reason Phil is needed is because he possesses psychic powers that the party might find useful, these being the equivalent of Philoctetes' bow. Phil, who is iconoclastic and open-minded, joined the party because he was concerned for others and because he was against the unfettered use of private property; he left the party because he wished to freely investigate 'certain powers of the mind', and 'to *think*, for the best'. But the party is interested only in the 'Total history' of Marxist theory, which corresponds to the Greek need to capture Troy.[19]

Smith stays close to the basic plot-line of Sophocles by having Leo (who worked with Phil's father) pretend that he has fallen out with O'Dea and left the party: 'I don't run with that crowd anymore'; 'I quit'.[20] Phil explains that he too had 'Trouble with the same man. Incompatibility', and attacks the doctrinaire nature of Marxism that is seen as just another religion:

> They mutter and rant about fulfilling the laws of history like a pack of Calvinists howling over the Ten Commandments. It's another bloody religion, bloody-minded and blood-soaked, the law revealed to Moses Marx, the gospel of the saviours Lenin and Mao, to abide by and observe down to the last jot and tittle.[21]

But O'Dea is, of course, also on the island – '*very much the tourist ... incapable of warmth*' – and his presence is divined by Phil, who refuses Leo's request to rejoin the party.[22]

But at the end of Act Two, the audience infers that Phil will join O'Dea and Leo in the party because of a novel and contemporary *deus ex machina* that corresponds to the appearance of Herakles in Sophocles. This involves the reproduction of the *Annunciation* by Leonardo da Vinci, which suggests a new beginning, and a poster of Che Guevara, which suggests radical left-wing action :

> Without Phil seemingly being aware of it, the Leonardo *Annunciation* and the Che Guevara poster become as it were luminous and pulsating; this is the Deus ex Machina, the unconscious influence which changes his decision.[23]

Meanwhile, Leo changes his view and attacks O'Dea's doctrinaire positions: 'History demands human sacrifices, and your savage philosophy – philosophy? Ha! –your savage religion rejoices in providing victims. You're not a Marxist, you're an Aztec.'[24] At which point, Phil enters and decides to rejoin the party, but with reservations: what his unconscious is 'after is not clear', and he remains opposed to O'Dea: 'I am with *ye* against *you*, O'Dea.'[25]

---

[1]. T.B.L. Webster, *Philoctetes* (Cambridge: Cambridge University Press, 1970); H.D.F. Kitto, *Form and Meaning in Drama* (London: Methuen, 1960); pp. 87-137; B.M.W. Knox, *The Heroic Temper* (Berkeley / Los Angeles: University of California Press, 1966), pp.117-42; M.W. Blundell, *Helping Friends and Harming Enemies* (Cambridge: Cambridge University Press, 1989), pp. 184-225, H. M. Roisman *Sophocles -Philoctetes* (London: Methuen, 2005).

[2] P. Vidal-Naquet in *Myth and Tragedy in Ancient Greece* (New York: Zone Books, 1990), pp. 161-79; l. Leda-Richards, *Ramus* 27(1998), pp. 1-26.

[3] B. Arkins in *The Languages of Ireland*, eds. M. Cronin and C. O Cuilleanain (Dublin: Four Courts Press, 2003), pp. 167-78.

[4] Desmond Egan, *Philoctetes* (Newbridge: Goldsmith Press, 1998), with comment by B. Arkins at pp. 5-10.

[5] Desmond Egan, *The Death of Metaphor* (Gerrards Cross: Colin Smythe, 1990), pp. 120-22.

[6] Virginia Woolf, quoted in T. Savory, *The Art of Translation* (London: Jonathan Cape), 1968, p. 60.

[7] Egan (note 4), pp. 16-17.

[8] Seamus Heaney, *The Cure at Troy* (London: Faber & Faber, 1990). For comment see C. Meir in *Studies in the Contemporary Irish Theatre*, eds. J. Genet and E. Hellegouarch (Caen: University of Caen Press, 1991), pp. 67-72; *id*. In *The Classical World and the Mediterranean*, eds. G. Serpillo and D. Badin (Cagliari: Universitá di Sassari, 1996), pp. 256-60; M. McDonald, *Classics Ireland* 3(1996), pp. 129-40; T. Eagleton in *Theatre Stuff: Critical Essays on Contemporary Irish*

Theatre, ed. E. Jordan (Dublin: Carysfort Press, 2000), pp. 172-75; H. Denard, *PAS: A Journal of Performance and Art 22*, 3(2000), pp. 1-18.

[9] Heaney, quoted in McDonald (note 8), p. 137.

[10] McDonald (note 8), 135; Heaney (note 8), p. 27.

[11] Heaney (note 8), p. 7; p. 5; pp. 6-7.

[12] Seamus Heaney in *Amid Our Troubles*, ed. M. McDonald and J.M. Walton (London: Methuen, 2002), p. 172.

[13] *ibid.*, p. 175.

[14] Heaney (note 8), p. 2.

[15] Heaney (note 12), p. 172.

[16] Heaney (note 8), pp. 77-81.

[17] Sydney Bernard Smith, *New and Selected Poems* (Dublin: Raven Press, 1984).

[18] Sydney Bernard Smith, *Sherca* (Newark: Proscenium Press, 1979).

[19] Smith (note 18), p. 15; p. 17; p. 18.

[20] *ibid.*, p. 13; p. 15.

[21] *ibid.*, p. 15; p. 18.

[22] *ibid.*, p. 5.

[23] *ibid.*, p. 28.

[24] *ibid.*, p. 34.

[25] *ibid.*, p. 35; p. 37.

6 | Sophocles' *Electra*

1

Sophocles' *Electra*[1] deals with the latter part of the story of the dysfunctional house of Atreus, 'a house of death if ever there was one'[2] (for which see Chapter Twelve). When the Greek leader Agamemnon comes here from Troy after a successful campaign, he is murdered by his wife Clytemnestra and her lover Aegisthus. This murder must be avenged by the children of the marriage, Orestes and Electra, so that *Electra* is a revenge play like *Hamlet*. Faithful to her father's memory, Electra is implacably hostile to Clytemnestra and Aegisthus, who bully her because of her constant mourning for Agamemnon. So although for most of the play Electra is not involved in the plotting of revenge, she is its focal point, and has one of the longest speaking parts in Athenian tragedy. But there is a clear contrast between brother and sister. Orestes is a man of the city-state (*polis*) who exists only for external action, for deeds (*erga*), and endorses statements, words (*logoi*) that promote action. Electra, a lonely Sophoclean hero, is trapped within the house (*oikos*) in a female world of lamentation, a type of statement (*logoi*) that inhibits action,[3] but which can nevertheless create shared memory, and social and familial unity.[4]

In Sophocles' *Electra*, Orestes arrives at Mycenae to avenge the murder of Agamemnon by stealth in obedience to the Delphic Oracle. But much must happen before this can be accomplished. After Clytemnestra has a bad dream in which Agamemnon returns to life, she and Electra exchange abuse in the language of the law-courts. Then Orestes' childhood attendant arrives to report the (fictitious) death of Orestes in the longest set-piece in the plays of Sophocles. This report, though false, demonstrates the powerful effect of speech (*logos*), causing Clytemnestra joy and Electra despair; at the same time, it paves the way for Orestes' revenge. Indeed Electra recovers, and determines to kill Clytemnestra and Aegisthus, so that she has now, as required, entered the world of men, the world of deeds (*erga*); her sister Chrysothemis refuses to help. Orestes and his friend Pylades appear, and gradually Orestes tells Electra who he is. The two men, with the help of Electra, kill Clytemnestra; here we see the truth of Virginia Woolf's dictum that the characters of Sophocles are 'decided, ruthless, direct'.[5] Finally, the chorus of Mycenaean women rejoice at the final passing of the curse of the house of Atreus.

The theme of Sophocles' *Electra* was also handled by Aeschylus in his tragedy *The Libation-Bearers* (458 BC), and by Euripides in his play *Electra*[6] (we do not know the exact dates of the plays by Sophocles and Euripides, or which came first). So, for once, we can analyse the different ways in which the three major tragedians of the fifth century treated the same myth, one basic difference being that Aeschylus dealt with Electra within the *Oresteia* trilogy that covers several generations of the family of Atreus, while Sophocles and Euripides concentrate on the individual figure of Electra in a single play. But the two later plays are very different: the Electra of Sophocles is a fully heroic figure, the Electra of Euripides is a mundane person who is married to a poor farmer, and endures great physical privation. Myth for Euripides is reduced to the level of everyday life.

The issue of Orestes' guilt after his killing of his mother is handled in distinct ways by the dramatists. In Aeschylus, Orestes feels remorse and becomes deranged; he is pursued by the Furies, avenging spirits who deal with murder in the family. In Sophocles, there is no question of Orestes feeling guilt, and he is not pursued by the Furies; his matricide is presented as a given without authorial comment. In Euripides, Orestes sees the potential murder of his mother as brutal, and has to have his resolve strengthened by Electra (who, after the matricide, is herself liable to guilt).

2

Frank McGuinness[7] is a leading contemporary dramatist who has achieved an international reputation with plays such as *Observe The Sons of Ulster Marching Towards the Somme*, *Mutabilitie* and *Carthaginians*. He has also engaged in a major appropriation of classic plays from the repertoire of Europe: Ibsen, Strindberg,

Chekhov, Lorca, Brecht. But McGuinness admits that 'I had never been able to get a handle on Greek theatre'. Until in 1997 he was commissioned to translate Sophocles' *Electra* by the director David Leveaux for the actress Zoe Wanamaker. Since *Electra* heavily stresses the character of Electra this chimed with several of McGuinness's plays such as *Bag lady*: 'In many respects, *Bag Lady* and *Electra* are both together, go hand in hand'. McGuinness wanted his *Electra*, which might adumbrate conflict in the Balkans and in Northern Ireland, to be modern: 'I did set out to write a play of *Electra*, based on the Greek, but that would be of its time, of the 1990s'. McGuinness therefore stresses how the human characters in *Electra* are 'absolutely responsible' for their own actions, that 'God is dead in *Electra*', and that these actions cause real pain that 'still can break an audience's heart'.[8] For McGuinness, Electra is single-minded and implacable, yet lonely and vulnerable (as seen in the stage-direction after the death of Orestes is announced: '*Electra howls*').[9]

What makes McGuinness's *Electra* a version rather than a translation is his use of language, his register and his syntax. McGuinness puts Sophocles' stylized Greek into modern English by using a register of language that is concise, unadorned, hard. As this extract from an early speech of Electra shows:[10]

> How do you think I survive the days when I see him,
> I see Aegisthus sitting on my father's throne?
> He wears every stitch my father wore.
> He pours wine on the same fire where he murdered.
> And the worst – what is worst –
> I see my father's bed, and his killer lies beside my mother.
> Mother – is that a fit name for such a woman?
> She is so depraved she lives with that obscenity
> She fears no face of retribution.
> It's as if she's gloating over what she's done.

This clarity is enhanced by a pervasive stylistic device that alters Sophocles' traditional syntax into that associated with free verse: McGuinness breaks down relatively long Greek sentences into brief English sentences or phrases, presented in very short lines and involving repetition, so that a phrase is no longer a phrase, but becomes a line of poetry.[11] The basic effect of all this is to hammer home the message. As in Electra's initial lament:[12]

> Divine light,
> Sweet air,
> Again hear

My pain.
Divine light,
Sweet air,
Again hear
My pain.
Have you witnessed when morning breaks
My heart break, my heart break?
When night falls, I do not feast
In this house of ghosts.
I lie alone.
My father's dead.
He did not lie on a foreign shore.
Here, at home,
My mother's hands turned red
With his blood. Adulteress,
Adulterer, she and Aegisthus
Split him open with an axe.

---

[1] For *Electra*, see J.H. Kells, *Sophocles Electra* (Cambridge : Cambridge University Press, 1973); Virginia Woolf in *Sophocles*, ed. T. Woodward (Englewood Cliffs, N.J.: Prentice Hall, 1966), pp.122-24; T. Woodward, *ibid.*, pp. 125-145; H.P. Foley, *Female Acts in Greek Tragedy* (Princeton/Oxford: Princeton University Press, 2001), pp. 145-71; M. Lloyd, *Sophocles: Electra* (London: Methuen 2005).

[2] E.F. Watling, *Sophocles – Electra and Other Plays* (Harmondsworth: Penguin, 1953), p. 69.

[3] Woodward (note 1), *passim.*

[4] Foley (note 1), p. 155.

[5] Woolf (note 1), p. 124.

[6] H.C. Baldry, *The Greek Tragic Theatre* (London: Chatto & Windus, 1971), pp. 109-28.

[7] Frank McGuinness, *Sophocles-Electra* (London: Faber & Faber, 1997). For Electra in Britain see E. Hall in *Sophocles Revisited: Essays Presented to Sir Hugh Lloyd-Jones* (Oxford: Oxford University Press, 1999). For the Electra of Hofmannsthal and Strauss see S. Goldhill, *Who needs Greek?* (Cambridge: Cambridge University Press, 2002), pp. 108-77.

[8] Frank McGuinness, interview with Joseph Long in *Amid Our Troubles*, eds. M.McDonald and J.M. Walton (London: Methuen, 2002), p. 263; p. 273; p. 264; p. 270; p. 274.

[9] McGuinness (note 8), p. 26.

[10] *ibid.*, p. 9.

[11] C. Scott in *Modernism*, ed. M. Bradbury and J. McFarlane (Harmondsworth: Penguin, 1985), p. 362.

[12] McGuinness (note 8), p. 4.

7 | Euripides' *Medea*

Euripides' *Medea*[1] deals with the later part of the myth of Jason and Medea, but to appreciate the tragedy fully we must be aware of the earlier section of that myth, which contains elements of folk-tale (*Märchen*). Having usurped the throne of Iolcus in Thessaly, Pelias deprived Jason of his inheritance as king, but promised to restore it to him if Jason brought back to Greece the Golden Fleece, which was located in Colchis at the eastern end of the Black Sea (modern Georgia), and was guarded by a dragon that never slept. Jason and some fifty heroes set out from Greece on the ship of the Argo, this voyage of the Argonauts being a very old example of quest-motif. Upon their arrival in Colchis, the king Aeetes said he would give Jason the Fleece if he performed various impossible tasks (such as yoking to a plough a pair of fire-breathing bulls). With the help of the king's daughter Medea ('the cunning one') – who was the granddaughter of the Sun and a skilled sorceress/poisoner – Jason accomplished these tasks. Medea then engineered the Argonauts' escape with the Fleece from Colchis, murdering her brother Apsyrtus in the process. She next persuaded Pelias' daughters to restore their father to youth by magic, but gave them ineffective herbs and so brought about his death. As a result, Jason and Medea had to leave Iolcus and seek refuge in Corinth. They live there as a married couple with two male children, until Jason decides to abandon Medea, and marry Glauce, daughter of the king Creon. Euripides' *Medea* dramatizes the resulting situation.

Medea is Euripides' most Sophoclean tragedy: no other play of his is constructed so firmly round a central character – like

Sophocles' Antigone or Electra. Medea dominates the action of the play throughout, and, though liable to extreme behaviour, is an authentic character who turns out to have an element of the superhuman. Jason, on the other hand, is neurotic because of his obsessive pursuit of the security that marriage into a Greek royal family offers; this leads him to exclude from his life sexuality (his relationship with Medea) and guilt (his failure to acknowledge he has abandoned her).[2] So this is no eternal triangle in the modern sense, in fact it constitutes the reverse: *Jason loved Medea, but just wishes to be married to Glauce.* This deviance in Jason's behaviour is mirrored in the deviant syntax of the Chorus' statement (line 18): 'Jason sleeps with a royal marriage'.[3]

Medea lends itself to analysis in terms of the binary oppositions of structuralism, with the overriding opposition being between the man Jason and the woman Medea. Beneath the umbrella of this man/woman conflict, there are the added polarities of custom (*nomos*) versus nature (*physis*); of city (*polis*) versus house (*oikos*); of marriage (*gamos*) versus sexual love (*eros*); of Greek versus foreigner. In other words, Jason stands for the public world of the Greek city and its value-system, which stresses marriage; Medea stands for the private world of the foreign person and her value-system, which stresses love.

These oppositions are brilliantly brought out by Euripides in a speech of Medea to the chorus of Corinthian women, and in a number of confrontations between Jason and Medea (the agon).[4] In what may be the most notable feminist statement in classical literature, Medea sums up her position by contrasting men at war with women giving birth (a very hazardous procedure in classical Greece): 'I would rather stand three times in the battle line than bear one child' (line 250-251).[5]

Medea is a revenge play.[6] But it is a revenge play of the type in which the aggrieved party (Medea) does not kill her antagonist (Jason), but rather that person's children and his new kin. When Creon seeks to exile her, Medea supplicates[7] him, and begs for one more day, which he agrees to. This allows Medea to engineer the deaths of Glauce and Creon by having her children bring them a poisoned robe and crown. Medea then proceeds to kill her own children in order to get at Jason, a motif that is probably the invention of Euripides[8] (she had been alerted to men's vulnerability in regard to children by King Aegeus of Athens, who finds himself unhappily childless, and who promises her sanctuary).[9] To perpetuate these unspeakable horrors Medea becomes a female intruder into a male world, one which she disrupts to devastating effect.[10]

Medea is then given sanctuary in Athens by Aegeus, brought there from Corinth in the chariot of the Sun-god. This quadruple murderess is endorsed by the gods and by the city of Athens, surely one of the most shocking statements ever made in the history of Athenian drama, something to send shivers down every male back during this very civic occasion in the Theatre of Dionysus, the god of paradox. This may be the reason that Euripides came third in the competition of 431 BC, but now *Medea* is very often seen as a major feminist statement, the tragic equivalent of Aristophanes' *Lysistrata*; for Medea is, precisely, a great woman.

2

Irish appropriation of Euripides' *Medea* follows the same pattern as that of Sophocles' *Philoctetes*: a straight translation, which is by Desmond Egan; a version, which is by Brendan Kennelly; and a loose adaptation, which is by Marina Carr.

Desmond Egan's translation of *Medea*[11] is a straight one that is made from the original Greek (which is included), with nothing added or subtracted; such adherence to Euripides forces us to interrogate the meaning of the Greek text – along the lines just presented – without recourse to any modern material. Indeed Egan has elsewhere commented on the meaning of *Medea*, seeing Medea as 'the first feminist heroine', and Jason as the 'prototype of the male chauvinist';[12] a view which his translation endorses (a further important aspect of Egan's translation is that it is suitable for use in Classical Civilization programmes in schools and universities, where it is a popular choice).

Egan's considerable achievement in translating *Medea* can be seen in both the episodes and the choral odes, where, in dealing with what he calls Euripides' 'virtuouso use of language',[13] he adopts an emphatic modern register that avoids both archaisms and neologisms. Compare Egan's vigorous verse translation of lines 488-98 with a recent prose translation by James Morwood. Here is Morwood:[14]

> And though, vilest of men, you reaped the benefits from me, you betrayed me, and made a new marriage – and this though we have children, since if you had still been without a child, it would have been pardonable for you to desire this match. No more is there any trusting to oaths, and I am at a loss to understand whether

you think that the gods you swore by then no longer rule or that
men now live by new standards of what is right – for well you
know that you have not kept your oaths to me. Alas for this right
hand which you often held, also for those knees – touched by an
evil man in an empty gesture – how we have missed our hopes.

And here is Egan:[15]

and having got all of this out of me, lowest of the low!
you betrayed me, found yourself a new bed
after our children were born. If you were still childless
your lusting for another bed might have been forgivable!
But no! Respect for our oath is forgotten. I wonder
do you imagine the ancient Gods no longer have power
and that new laws apply to humans nowadays?
because I know you are a perjurer in my regard.
Poor right hand which you often took hold of
And these knees – how vainly were they clung-to by an evil man!
I was disappointed in all my hopes.

The choral odes in Athenian tragedy are notoriously difficult, but
here too Egan is very successful in his translation, avoiding
translatorese of the type parodied by Ezra Pound in his *Homage to
Sextus Propertius*: 'O couch made happy by my long delectations'.[16]
This is his accomplished translation of part of the third choral ode
about the glorious city of Athens (lines 824-4):[17]

Happy the Athenians, son of Erechtheus, of old!
born of the blessed gods, in a sacred, unconquered land,
taking their nourishment from
supreme Wisdom always moving gracefully
through the luminous air. There, once upon a time, it is said
the Nine Pierian Muses, the pure ones
gave birth to golden Harmony.

A people sprung, too, from the waters of the smooth-flowing
Cephisus, where they say that Aphrodite of Cypris drew water
breathing gentle breaths of wind on the land;
where, too, those Loves, companions of Wisdom
and co-workers in all hands of goodness,
escort Aphrodite, constantly strewing on her hair
perfumed garlands of rose.

3

Brendan Kennelly's version of *Medea*,[18] which was first staged in
Dublin in 1988 and toured England in 1989, keeps the invariant
core of Euripides' plot, but greatly expands the original from 1419
lines to 2,242 lines. Like *Antigone*, *Medea* affords Kennelly the
opportunity to draw another portrait of 'powerful women

confronting organized male power', of women countering the
negative effects of patriarchal culture. For Kennelly, Medea 'speaks
for all women who have ever been ditched':[19] the cry/of the first
woman. Betrayed by the first man'.[20] This archetypal role that
Medea plays links up both with Kennelly's own personal life and
with wider concerns about society in Ireland. Kennelly is on record
as identifying with women who provide him with a form of female
knowledge, and as being a person who has experienced separation
and divorce. At the same time, Kennelly's *Medea* should be read
against the reality of marital breakdown in Ireland, and the debates
about divorce that took place in the 1980s and 90s (it became legal
in 1997). As Tony Harrison writes:[21]

> Beneath *all* Greek mythology
> are struggles between HE and SHE
> that we're still waging.
> In every quiet suburban wife
> dissatisfied with married life
> is MEDEA, raging!

Rage is indeed the key word for Kennelly, the sentiment of
Medea abandoned by Jason : 'The world/Medea's world. The world
of rage'.[22] As she seeks to educate men, Medea waxes eloquent in
demotic language about the sexual domination of women by men:[23]

> Men, the horny despots of our bodies,
> sucking, fucking, licking, chewing, farting into our skin,
> sitting on our faces, fingering our arses,
> exploring our cunts, widening our thighs,
> drawing the milk that gave the bastards life.

But as the organization of fifth century Athens shows, sex is not
just personal, it is political: 'Kings will be strong on thrones/if they
are uppermost in bed'. And art too can portray sexual power: 'There
will be songs/to celebrate the terrific truth/of women. There will
be/womansongs in answer to the false/songs of men'; at that time
when 'honour/will be paid to women'.[24]

Medea sets out to overthrow Jason's world of male lies: 'The
time has come/ to turn Jason's world upside down/ and inside out'.
Medea can achieve this because she is not just a woman scorned,
but a kind of earth-spirit who is identified with natural forces like
sun, clouds, and rain, and who has a cry 'like the cry of Nature
itself'; as Jason says, 'There's a demon in you.'[25] Normal standards
do not apply to demonic forces of this order, and so, when the

Chorus end the play by asking 'Is Medea's crime Medea's glory?' the answer has to be 'yes'.[26]

4

Marina Carr's play *By the Bog of Cats...*, which was first staged at the Abbey Theatre in October 1998 and is set in the Irish Midlands, is a loose adaptation of Euripides' *Medea*.[27] Carr sees a general relationship between theatre audiences at the present time and those in fifth century Athens: 'I think the people have never been more open since, possibly, the Greek world'.[28] Very specifically, Carr links *By the Bog of Cats...* to Euripides: 'The plot is completely *Medea*. It was surprising how few people picked up on that initially'.[29] But the theatre director M.K. Martinovich held of her staging of this play that 'Familiarity with the *Medea* myth played a crucial part in the production's development'.[30] Carr does indeed achieve a very Greek tone in *By the Bog of Cats...*; as Frank McGuinness says, 'I am certain in this play she writes in Greek'.[31] Hence Olwen Fouéré, who played the Medea-figure, Hester Swane, in the play's premiere, noted that 'Hester is a very mythical character, archetypal in a sense'.[32]

Hester Swane (aged 40) has spent fourteen years of her life with Carthage Kilbride, whom she regards as her husband – 'I'm not talking about love... Our bond is harder' – and she has a child by him named Josie (age 7); Carthage's mother calls her 'Hester Swane's little bastard'.[33] Carthage now proposes to abandon Hester and marry Caroline Cassidy (aged 20), who is the daughter of a prosperous landowner. Such a marriage will make Carthage respectable and the pillar of the community, whereas Hester, as a traveller, is an outsider in Irish society – as Medea from Colchis was in Greece; as Carr says, 'I chose to make her a traveller because travellers are our national outsiders, aren't they?'[34] The further suggestion that Hester is a witch – 'whoosin' by on her broom' and practising that 'black art thing' – corresponds to Medea's power as a sorceress.[35] Then it is Hester who (like Medea) has given Carthage his current position: 'It was me who told him he could do no better. It was my money that bought him his first five acres.'[36] Indeed Hester, like Medea, killed her brother with Carthage's help and stole his money. One aspect of Medea is here transferred to Xavier Cassidy, the bride's father: just as Medea places poison on the dress and crown she gives to her rival Glauce, so Cassidy gives his son's dog strychrine, so that, when the boy embraces the dog, he too is poisoned.

At the beginning of *By the Bog of Cats...*, Carthage, who 'never grew his backbone', is abandoning Hester and Josie 'for a few lumpy auld acres and notions of respectability', and tells her, like Creon, that 'I want you out of here before dusk'. But Hester refuses to leave, and asserts herself strongly: 'If you think I'm going to let you walk over me like that, ya don't know me at all'; ominously, she involves the child Josie in her anger, telling Carthage that, if he goes through with the wedding, 'you'll never see Josie again'.37

Like Medea, Hester Swane moves out of the private world of her relationship with Carthage Kilbride into the public world and with devastating effect. But Carr's ending in *By the Bog of Cats...* is substantially different from that of Euripides' Medea. Hester exacts her revenge on Carthage by burning down his house and the animals attached to it. She then proceeds to kill her daughter with a knife, as Medea kills her two children. But whereas Medea's murders were part of a revenge upon Jason, Hester's killing of Josie is an act of love that seeks to prevent the child from being abandoned by her mother.38 Hester's own fate is even more different: far from being rescued by divine forces and given sanctuary elsewhere, Hester commits suicide (like the Mai and Portia Coughlan, in their name-plays). Since both Hester and Josie cry 'Mam – Mam' at the moment of death, their close connection is stressed.39

Carr here gives a significant new twist to the Medea theme. Writing as a woman about women, Carr deconstructs the currently dominant reading of Euripides' *Medea* as a feminist statement, in which Medea's revenge through infanticide is vindicated. Hester Swane is not vindicated, but dies by her own hand; she who lives by the knife will die by the knife. If Hester Swane is a feminist icon, she is a very different one from Medea.

---

1 For the Medea myth and its subsequent history see J.J. Clauss and S.I. Johnston (eds.), *Medea, Essays on Medea in Myth, Literature, Philosophy, and Art* (Princeton: Princeton University Press, 1997); E. Hall, F. Macintosh and O. Taplin (eds.), *Medea in Performance 1500-2000* (Oxford: Oxford University Press, 2000); S. Joseph, *Medea in late Twentieth Century Theatre: Ancient Sources and Recent Transformations* (Diss. Washington 2002); E. Griffiths, *Medea*

(London: Methuen, 2006). For commentaries on Euripides' *Medea* see M.L. Page, *Euripides' Medea* (Oxford: Oxford University Press, 1978); M.J. Mastronarde, *Euripides-Medea* (Cambridge: Cambridge University Press, 2002), with Bibliography at pp. 398-416.

2 W. Sole, *Existentialism and Euripides* (Berwick, Vic.: Aureal Publications, 1977), pp. 13-34.

3 B. Arkins, *Ramus* 11(1982), p. 120.

4 M. Lloyd, *The Agon in Euripides* (Oxford: Oxford University Press, 1992).

5 Translation by J. Morwood in *Euripides – Medea and other plays* (Oxford: Oxford University Press, 1998), p. 7.

6 A.P. Burnett, *Classical Philology* 68(1973), pp. 1-24; *id.*, *Revenge in Attic and Later Tragedy* (Berkeley/Los Angeles: University of California Press, 1998).

7 For supplication see J. Gould, *Journal of Hellenic Studies* 93(1973), pp. 74-103; also in his *Myth, ritual, memory, and exchange: essays in Greek Literature and culture* (Oxford: Oxford University Press, 2001), pp. 22-77.

8 P.E. Easterling, *Yale Classical Studies* 25(1977), pp. 177-91.

9 E. Schlesinger, *Hermes* 94(1966), pp. 26-53 = *Euripides*, ed. E. Segal (Englewood Cliffs, N.J.: Prentice-Hall, 1968), pp. 70-89.

10 M. Shaw, *Classical Philology* 70(1975), pp. 255-66.

11 Desmond Egan, *Euripides – Medea* (Laurinburg/Newbridge: St. Andrews Press/The Kavanagh Press, 1990).

12 Desmond Egan, *The Death of Metaphor* (Gerrards Cross: Colin Smythe, 1990), p. 122.

13 *ibid.*

14 Morwood (note 5), p. 14.

15 Egan (note 11), p. 31.

16 Ezra Pound in J.P. Sullivan, *Ezra Pound and Sextus Propertius* (London: Faber & Faber, 1965), p. 143.

17 Egan (note 11), pp. 42-43.

18 Brendan Kennelly, *Euripides' Medea – A New Version* (Newcastle-upon-Tyne: Bloodaxe, 1991). For comment see K. McCracken in *Dark Fathers into Light: Brendan Kennelly*, ed. R. Pine (Newcastle-upon-Tyne: Bloodaxe, 1994), pp. 131-39; M. McDonald in Clauss and Johnston (note 1), pp. 305-12; J. McDonagh in *Amid Our Troubles – Irish Versions of Greek Tragedy* ed. M. McDonald and J.M. Walton (London: Methuen, 2002), pp. 213-31; Joseph (note 1), pp. 85-97; J. McDonagh, *Brendan Kennelly – A Host of Ghosts* (Dublin: The Liffey Press, 2004), pp. 107-26.

19 Kennelly, quoted in Joseph (note 1), p. 86; p. 92.

20 Kennelly (note 18), p. 21.

21 Tony Harrison, *Dramatic Verse 1973-1985* (Newcastle-upon-Tyne: Bloodaxe, 1985), p. 371.

22 Kennelly (note 18), p. 20.

23 *ibid.*, p. 25.

24 *ibid.*, p. 13; p. 34; p. 33.

25 *ibid.*, p. 45; p. 21; p. 72; p. 75.

26 'Yes' is advocated by McDonald (note 18), p. 131 and McDonagh, 2004, p. 119; 'no' is advocated by McCracken (note 18), p. 138.

27 Text of *By the Bog of Cats...* in Marina Carr, *Plays One* (London: Faber & Faber, 1999), pp. 257-341; also Marina Carr, *By the Bog of Cats...* (Oldcastle: Gallery Press, 1998). For comment on Carr see *The Theatre of Marina Carr: 'before rules was made'*, eds. C. Leeney and A. McMullan (Dublin: Carysfort Press, 2003); for *By the Bog of Cats...* in relationship to Euripides' *Medea* see in Leeney and McMullan Index s.v. 'Euripides', E. Jordan in McDonald and Walton (note 18), pp. 243-62. For the further classical influence of Seneca see Joseph (note 1), p. 172.

28 Marina Carr in *Theatre Talk*, eds. L. Chambers, G. Fitzgibbon and E. Jordan (Dublin: Carysfort Press, 2001), p. 57.

29 Marina Carr in Reading the Future: Irish Writers in Conversation with Mike Muphy, ed. C. Ni Anluain, Dublin: RTE, 2000, p. 51.

30 M.K. Martinovich in Leeney and McMullan (note 27), p. 119.

31 Frank McGuinness, *ibid.*, p. 88.

32 Olwen Fouéré, *ibid.*, p. 161.

33 Marina Carr 1999 (note 27), p. 269; p. 279.

34 Marina Carr in Leeney and McMullan (note 27), p. 178.

35 Marina Carr 1999 (note 27), p. 270; p. 324.

36 *ibid.*, p. 284.

37 *ibid.*, p. 289; p. 290; p. 288; p. 289.

38 Olwen Fouéré in Leeney and McMullan (note 27), pp. 166-67.

39 Marina Carr, 1999 (note 27), p. 339; p. 341.

8 | Euripides' *Bacchae*

1

Central to Euripides' great play *The Bacchae*, first produced in 405 BC, is the god Dionysus[1], who was an intruder into Greece from the barbarous recesses of Thrace and Phrygia. The Orphic form of Dionysus' myth runs as follows: when Dionysus Zagreus was born from the union of Zeus and Persephone, Hera, the wife of Zeus, was jealous and incited the Titans to tear Dionysus to pieces and devour him; but the virgin goddess Athene rescued the heart of Dionysus and brought it to Zeus, who swallowed it and was therefore able to beget Dionysus later on Semela, when he came to her in the form of lightning. It is the latter part of the myth that is found in *The Bacchae*. A cycle of birth, death and resurrection is central not only to the myth of Dionysus, but also to his ritual worship, so that he is, in part, a vegetation god who dies and rises again in the spring. Dionysus was not a transcendent deity living on Mount Olympus, but the god of wild, mysterious nature and consequently of the emotional, irrational side of human life. Dionysus is also, as a transforming force, the god of wine, of the theatre and of the mask, so that it is appropriate for Euripides to deal with him in this late play *The Bacchae*.

The Bacchae stresses the fact that it is women in particular who worship the god Dionysus (Bacchae are women followers of Bacchus, another name for Dionysus). Every second year at midwinter he was worshipped in a festival at Delphi by Bacchae, who practised an ecstatic mountain dance culminating in the tearing to pieces of an animal (*sparagmos*) and the eating of its raw flesh (*omophagia*). This sacramental meal brought the participants into communion with the god. It is not surprising therefore that in his list of four types of divine madness Plato included the madness inspired by Dionysus and that Louis MacNeice regarded his worship as epitomizing the irrationality of the normally rational Greeks; At one level, then, *The Bacchae* provides an aetiological explanation of how the cult of Dionysus came to Greece (The power of Dionysus is also shown by the Chorus of Lydian women who embody the threatened cult through music, song and dance, but who also stress moderation). These Bacchae are both a collective unit (*thiasos*) and a group of individual women, each of whom has her own part to play.[2]

> Models of logic and lucidity, dignity, sanity
> The golden mean between opposing ills
> Though they were exception of course but only exceptions
> The bloody Bacchands on the Thracian hills.

The situation in *The Bacchae* arises out of the fact that in Thebes false stories about Dionysus' birth have been spread and that the king Pentheus (whose name means 'grief') has rejected the worship of Dionysus. This god of unbounded personality has therefore initiated many Theban women – including Agave, the mother of Pentheus – into secret Bacchic rites: on Mount Cithaeron, they are engaged in the ecstatic worship of Dionysus, brandishing the thyrsus, a wand with ivy leaves attached to its tip, and wearing fawnskins entwined with snakes; from blows of the thyrsus, wine, honey, milk and water flow; the women suckle animals and conquer men.

But the stress in *The Bacchae* is very clearly on the clash between the king Pentheus and the god Dionysus, who uniquely in Greek tragedy appears throughout the play: the fact that the Bacchae have left the city and are worshipping the god in the mountains is something he finds intolerable and proposes to remedy. In a typical male fantasy, Pentheus sees Bacchic worship as simply an excuse for drink and sex, so that he is opposed to the rites of Aphrodite, the goddess of love[3], as well as to those of Dionysus. This clash between the irrational religion of Dionysus and the extreme rationalism of Pentheus can be formulated in a number of binary oppositions under the general umbrella Dionysus versus Pentheus: emotion v. reason; nature (*physis*) v. custom (*nomos*); animal versus human; the mountains v. the city; exuberance v. restraint; female worshippers v. male king. But Dionysus is backed by Pentheus' grandfather Cadmus and by the blind prophet

Tiresias, always in Greek tragedy a source of truth (this has a comic aspect).

Pentheus debates with Dionysus and appears to hold his own, but he can be no match for the god in human shape: when Dionysus is captured, he escapes and symbolically destroys Pentheus' palace.[4] While Pentheus is specially dependent on buildings, Dionysus is not bound by architectural structures.[5] Dionysus then exhibits his control over Pentheus by drawing on the king's subconscious, voyeuristic wish to view the Bacchae and ensuring that he dresses like a woman to do so (transvestism is a well-known feature of initiatory religion in Greece); Dodds writes of 'the dark puritan whose passion is compounded of horror and unconscious desire'.[6] Furthermore, Pentheus appears to have a subconscious desire for his mother Agave:[7] he fantasizes about her making love, wants to spy on her doing so, wants to be carried in her arms. At the same time, the scene in which Pentheus views the Bacchae involves a meditation on the experience of theatre: the spectator is required to watch an impersonation, to accept a world that is not really there, something stressed by the fact that in the original production the Bacchae were played by men.[8]

At the climax of the play, Pentheus is torn to pieces like a scapegoat, like a sacrificial lamb by the Bacchae, including his mother Agave, who is deranged and thinks he is an animal;[9] she is responsible for the appalling crimes of human sacrifice, infanticide and cannibalism. In the first account of an insight and recall psychotherapy, Cadmus ensures that Agave is brought back step by step to inescapable reality.[10] But Cadmus, who himself did not worship Dionysus in an authentic way, is banished from Thebes – as is Agave.

The Bacchae is one of Euripides' greatest achievements in tragedy: the Parodos (the opening statement of the Chorus) provides a magnificent account of the worship of Dionysus; two brilliant Messenger speeches deal with the women's revels on Mount Cithaeron (the lull before the storm) and with the shocking death of Pentheus; specially dramatic is the moment when Pentheus is persuaded to spy on the Bacchae. Yet the meaning of the play is by no means clear-cut.

For the clash between Pentheus and Dionysus is not nearly so straightforward as that between Jason and Medea. As the play ponders the question 'What is wisdom?' what can be said is that the irrational as represented by Dionysus *must* be accommodated in human life. Failure to accept the significance of the irrational is itself a form of madness; as Tiresias says to Pentheus, 'Before this you were out of your mind. Now you are altogether mad'.[11] Nevertheless, a form of the irrational that runs out of control must be deprecated: the brutal killing of Pentheus by the Bacchae is too high a price to pay. A reasonable irrationality, so to speak, is required.

2

Transferred to Africa in Wole Soyinka's play *The Bacchae* and to America in Donna Tartt's novel *The Secret History*,[12] Euripides' tragedy *The Bacchae* has been appropriated in Ireland by Colin Teevan's translation *The Bacchai*, Derek Mahon's version *The Bacchae*, and Shaw's loose adaptation *Major Barbara*.

Colin Teevan is the author of a number of original plays such as *The Big Sea* and *Vinegar and Brown Paper*, and of translations such as *Manfridi's Cuckoos*. Teevan's appropriation of *The Bacchae*[13] – given the more obviously Greek title *Bacchai* – is called 'A new translation', and, apart from Euripides' text, includes only a six page Introduction by Edith Hall,[14] a short Appendix about a proposed secret language for the Chorus (which 'never quite made it to the final text'), and some additional material inserted into the play's fragmentary end. Stressing how accessible Euripides is, Hall in her Introduction shows how Dionysus and Pentheus have a 'transformed consciousness', because Dionysus, the god of drama, is a stage director as well as an actor, and because Pentheus renounces reality and becomes deluded. Hall further stresses the importance of the mask in Euripidean tragedy and of having just three actors play all the parts, with Teevan's play encompassing these aspects:[15]

> A major reason for the coherent vision and integrity of Colin Teevan's rendering of *Bacchai*, commissioned for performance by the National Theatre in London, is that at every stage in its evolution it has been envisaged as an acting text for realization not only in masks, but (as in the original production of Euripides' masterpiece in 405 BC) by no more than three actors.

Hence in Teevan's play, the same actor plays both Pentheus and Agave, which heightens the family drama to a great extent. Again, Teevan's adherence to Euripides' original stresses the fact that *The Bacchae* 'does not offer a single, simple way of understanding an incomprehensible universe.[16]

Teevan varies his style in *Bacchai*: the episodes make use of a long line, while the Choral odes are presented in a short lyric line. A passage from the Messenger's report about the Bacchae will serve to illustrate Teevan's achievement in the episodes. Here is Morwood's prose translation:[17]

> Some of them held a roe deer or wild wolf-cubs in their arms and all the recent mothers, whose breasts were still swollen for the offspring they had abandoned, gave to these their white milk. They put on garlands of ivy, of oak, and of flower-clustered bryony. And one of them took her thrysus and struck it against a rock, from which the dewy wetness of water lept forth. Another plunged her fennel rod into the earth's surface, and for her the god spurted up a spring of wine. Then all who felt a longing for the white drink scraped at the ground with their fingertips and took jets of milk in her hands. And from their ivy-clad thrysi dripped sweet streams of honey.

And here is Teevan's verse:[16]

> Those who'd left their newborn babes at home
> Took up in their arms wild fawns of the whelps of wolves
> Which they suckled to their milk-laden breasts.
> All wore wreaths of ivy or of oak leaf.
> One took her ivy-covered shaft and struck a rock
> And from it sprang a spring of fresh water,
> Another dug her shaft into the ground
> And out flew a fountain of the god's own wine
> If one wanted milk, she just scratched the earth
> With fingers, and the earth flowed with it
> While from each sacred shaft honey poured.

A good example of Teevan's lapidary style in the lyric passages is found in the Parodos:[19]

> Then spills the earth with milk
> Spills with wine, with honey
> Of wild bears, it spills forth:
> You are now Bacchai.
> And the priest lifts up
> His ivy-covered club
> Which burns with smoke as sweet
> An Asian frankincense.
> You run and dance around
> His now streaming torch,
> His hair a shock of flames
> As her roars you on;
> 'Go you Bacchai, go!
> With the gold of Mount Tmolus
> Beating in your heart.

> Sing Evoe to Dionysus,
> Sing Evoe to the god...'

Given that the end of *The Bacchae* is fragmentary (there may be a gap of 50 lines), Teevan adds an exchange between Cadmus and Agave about Pentheus, when Agave says 'I have killed him, yes, but I'm his mother still'. He also adds material to Dionysus' last major speech: 'Do not deny me./Do not insult me. Do not deride my arts,/My gifts. Do not attempt to silence me./Do not think that if you lock me up,/I will go away'.[20]

Finally, Teevan provides an excellent rendering of *The Bacchae's* formulaic ending, adding in the last line a reference to modern theatrical practice:[21]

> The gods take many forms,
> The gods move in strange ways,
> That which seemed, does not transpire
> And that which did not, does.
> This is what transpired here.
> Turn out the lights.

3

Derek Mahon's appropriation of *The Bacchae* is a version, styled by him as 'after Euripides' (he has also produced versions of Moliere's *The School for Husbands* – called *High Time* – and *The School for Wives*).[22] Mahon's view of the binary oppositions in *The Bacchae* is indicated by his three substantial epigraphs from Nietzsche, E.R. Dodds and Louis MacNeice. The epigraph from Nietzsche's *The Birth of Tragedy* introduces that work's famous distinction between Dionysus and Apollo, and stresses the way those gods interpenetrate each other within the individual person; the lesson seems to be that no person is wholly rational or wholly irrational:[23]

> Only so much of the Dionysian sub-stratum of the universe may enter an individual consciousness as can be dealt with by the Apollonian transfiguration; so that these two prime agencies must develop in strict proportion and in accordance with the principles of eternal justice. Whenever the Dionysian forces become too obstreperous, as is the case today, we are safe in assuming that Apollo is close at hand, though wrapped in a cloud, and that the rich effects of his beauty will be witnessed by a later generation.

Taken from E.R.Dodds' justly celebrated book *The Greeks and the Irrational*, Mahon's second epigraph asserts that Bacchae existed both in the Greek world and in the world of today, so that they must be dealt with by contemporary authorities:[24]

I have tried to show that Euripides' description of Maenadism is not to be accounted for in terms of the imagination alone; that inscriptional evidence reveals a closer relationship with actual cult than scholars have realized; and that the Maenad, however mythical certain of her acts, is not in essence a mythological character but an observed and still observable human type. Dionysus still has his votaries or victims, though we call them by other names; and Pentheus was confronted by a problem which other civil authorities have had to face in real life.

Louis MacNeice provides Mahon's third epigraph, in which he emphasizes the fact that Euripides (like Yeats) was very creative in his old age and that his previous apparent rationalism is counteracted by *The Bacchae*:[25]

Yeats's efflorescence in old age is perhaps unique in recent poetry. We might compare Euripides who, after a long life spent in struggling with and digesting new ideas, in gradually formulating a sceptical, rationalist attitude had in his old age the elasticity to admit that there was a case for Dionysus. Expanding on MacNeice in section ix of his poem 'The Yellow Book', Mahon observes that the forces represented by Dionysus are irresistible, that they must be afforded their due just as much as the Sophists that Euripides drew on earlier, and that the modern appearance of Dionysus has an earthy aspect that involves a rejection of the sublime;[26]

and look at the old age of Euripides

who, after a lifetime struggling with new ideas,
sent out his Bacchae to the woods and glens
to dance devotion to the god of vines
under the rocks, under the moonlit pines.
Bring on ivy and goatskin, pipe and drum
for Dionysus son of Semele is come
to release us from our servitude to the sublime ...

Mahon keeps the invariant core of the plot of *The Bacchae*, together with the structure of episodes and choral odes, but sometimes compresses the original: while the Parodes in Euripides runs to 93 lines, in Mahon it takes just 60 lines and is granted a refrain: 'Pipe and drum, pipe and drum;/let Thebes know Dionysus, son of Semele is come!'[27] At the end of *The Bacchae*, on the other hand, Mahon expands considerably on the rather bland comments of the Chorus on what has transpired, and uses another refrain from a popular song to stress the message: 'It's still the same old story,/a fight for love and glory,/and every heart admits that this is so'.[28]

Mahon makes explicit and makes modern the fundamental concerns of *The Bacchae*. Dionysus sums up the basic clash: 'there will be war between the Bacchant wives/and the strict spirit that controls their lives'. A spirit despised by the blind prophet Tiresias: 'I can't abide our rational theology'. But Pentheus exhibits the prejudices of Athenian men about women: 'The whole thing's an excuse for drink and sex'. Then the murder of Pentheus, though not justified, shows that reason is very limited, and can be literally dismembered: the Bacchae 'played "catch" with raw pieces of Pentheus' flesh'. Yet the Dionysian element in the human person will not be denied: 'let Thebes know Dionysus, son of Semele, is come.'[29]

Mahon skilfully modulates tone in *The Bacchae*. To the great set pieces Mahon brings a poet's touch and, at times, compassion; compare part of the Messenger's speech about the death of Pentheus in Morwood's prose translation and in Mahon's verse. Here is Morwood:[30]

> They set their innumerable hands on the fir and tore it up from the ground. Perched on high, he hurtled from his high seat down to the ground and as he fell, he poured out innumerable cries of sorrow, Pentheus the sorrowful. For he was learning that he was close to disaster. His mother, as priestess, was the first to begin the slaughter and she fell upon him. But he flung the band from his head so that the wretched Agave could recognize and not kill him, and he touched her cheek, saying: 'It's me, mother, your son Pentheus, whom you bore in the house of Echin. O mother, pity me and do not kill me for I have done wrong. I am your son'.

And here is Mahon:[31]

> A thousand hands took hold of the pine-tree
> and tore it from the earth; so Pentheus fell
> with a great scream, knowing the end was nigh.
> He flung his veil and hair aside and cried,
> 'Mother, I am your son Pentheus;
> you won't, for God's sake, kill your only child?'

Rhyme and half-rhyme is used freely by Mahon and can serve to stress the content (a considerable achievement at this point in English literary history):

> Pentheus, a rational, pretentious man,
> refuses to acknowledge who I am,
> denies the god heed I shall demonstrate
> to him and all the people of this state.

But rhyme can also be used to produce an ironic, distancing effect (as often in Mahon's poetry):[32]

> Excuse me, I must join the Bacchic dames
> On Mount Cithaeron where they play their games.

Occasional use of colloquial language is also effective : Pentheus exclaims 'Oh, for fuck's sake', and Dionysus calls Pentheus 'you pompous twit'[33]. On the other hand, Mahon's choral odes exhibit a 'clarity and grace' that lingers 'hauntingly over the scenes of human folly and divine anger':[34]

> Oh, to be on white
> Aphrodite's isle
> where love enchants the night
> for a brief mortal while
> and a thousand rivers flow
> into the sands below.
> Oh, to be where the airy
> slopes of Olympus sweep
> down to Pieria where
> the nine Muses sleep.
> Take us there, Dionysus,
> where ecstasy isn't banned
> and the holy thrysus
> sprouts from every hand!

4

Shaw's play *Major Barbara* (1905)[35] is a loose adaptation of *The Bacchae* that transposes ancient religious drama into modern dress and the social sphere. Dionysus becomes a very wealthy manufacturer of arms, Undershaft, who despises the current *status quo* in society and who has idealistic proposals to abolish property; he is therefore an example of the Life Force, in Shaw's words 'diabolical, subtle, and gentle, self-possessed, powerful and stupendous'.[36] The role of Pentheus is played in different ways by Barbara of the Salvation Army, and by Cusins (a Professor of Greek who is to marry her); they oppose Undershaft, but are eventually converted to his views. So to Cusins as Euripides a new Dionysus has appeared: 'Dionysus Undershaft has descended. I am possessed'.[37] The Salvation Army, which represents the Bacchae, is ambivalent. Though the Salvation Army 'reveals the true worship of Dionysus' and though Barbara is akin to Dionysus in her role as converter, the Army is initially compromised by its acceptance of the *status quo* in society. But when the Commissioner, Mrs.Baines, takes money from Undershaft, she becomes one of the Bacchae, and we witness 'the conversion of the Salvation Army to the worship of Dionysus'. Indeed the Army engages in a Bacchic revel: 'it marches to fight the devil with trumpet and drum, with music and dancing, with banner and palm, as becomes a sally from heaven by its leppy garrison'. Equally well, Undershaft acknowledges the role of Dionysus as god of wine: 'It makes life bearable to millions of people who could not endure their existence if they were quite sober'; as does Cusins: 'I think it was Dionysus who made me drunk.'[38]

Major Barbara is deeply indebted to Gilbert Murray,[39] who had been Professor of Greek at Glasgow. Shaw's play was written shortly after Murray's translation of *The Bacchae* was published in 1902, which Shaw saw as coming 'into our dramatic literature with all the impulsive power of an original book', and *Major Barbara* 'stands indebted' to Murray 'in more ways than one'. For Shaw based his Professor of Greek, Cusins, on Murray (he is constantly called 'Euripides'); used Murray's Euripides verses in the second act; accepted Murray's suggestion that Undershaft should be a representative of cosmic forcers rather than a free agent; and makes Cusins echo Murray when he says of Barbara: 'Dionysus and all the others are in herself.'[40]

Though religion is prominent in *Major Barbara* in the shape of the Salvation Army, the main issue is that of poverty and how it might be eradicated: Shaw argues that 'the greatest of our evils, and the worst of our crimes is poverty, and that our first duty, to which every other consideration should be sacrificed, is not to be poor'; Undershaft says 'I hate poverty and slavery worse than any other crimes whatsoever'.[41] Just as *The Bacchae* treats Dionysiac religion as highly problematic, so Shaw makes the solution to the problem of poverty deeply controversial by turning the manufacturer Undershaft into a philanthropist whose vast money solves the problem. And Undershaft has a Greek source for his ideas because he parodies Plato on philosophers and politicians (*Republic* 473 d): Plato's assertion that 'there will be no end to the troubles of states.... til philosophers becomes kings in the world or til we now call kings and rulers really and truly become philosophers'[42] turns into 'Plato says, my friend, that society cannot be saved until either the Professors of Greek take to making gunpowder or else the makers of gunpowder become Professors of Greek'.[43]

It is true that Euripides becomes for Shaw an enabling force: it is because Shaw follows the Greek dramatist in insisting on the irresistible power of Dionysus/Undershaft that he is able to move beyond the play's opening categories to a workable solution – as in many plays he was not.[44] Nevertheless, the solution adopted by Shaw is deeply controversial: it initially suggests a Wildean or, better, a Blakean paradox about a moral issue; closer examination establishes the immorality of Undershaft's position. The manufacture of weapons of mass destruction cannot be moral, even if the profits from it go to alleviate poverty. As Undershaft's wife, Lady Britomart, puts it with admirable common sense: he was 'always clever and unanswerable when he was defending nonsense and wickedness'.[45]

---

[1] For Dionysus see W.F. Otto, *Dionysus, Myth and Cult* (Bloomington: Indiana University Press, 1965). For editions of *The Bacchae* see E.R. Dodds, *Euripides' Bacchae* (Oxford: Oxford University Press, 1960); R. Seaford, *Euripides' Bacchae* (Warminster: Aris & Phillips, 1996), for comment see R.P. Winnington-Ingram, *Euripides and Dionysus – An Interpretation of the Bacchae* (London: Bristol Classical Press, 2003).

[2] Plato, *Phaedrus* 265 B (the three other forms of madness relate to prophecy, poetry and sex); *The Collected Poems of Louis MacNeice*, ed. E.R. Dodds (London: Faber & Faber, 1979), p. 118.

[3] W. Sale, *Existentialism and Euripides* (Berwick: Aureal Publications, 1977), pp. 110-15.

[4] S. Goldhill, *Reading Greek Tragedy* (Cambridge: Cambridge University Press, 1986), pp. 277-84.

[5] W.C. Scott, *TAPA* 105(1975), pp. 339-43.

[6] Dodds (note 1), *ad* pp. 222-23.

[7] Sale (note 3), pp. 115-16.

[8] H. Foley, *Ritual Irony: Poetry and Sacrifice in Euripides* (Ithaca/London: Cornell University Press, 1985), pp. 205-58.

[9] Lycurgus, king of the Edones in Thrace, also died after persecuting Dionysus; Aeschylus wrote on this topic.

[10] G. Dereveux, *JHS* 90(1970), pp. 35-48.

[11] Translated by J. Morwood, *Euripides – Bacchae and Other Plays* (Oxford: Oxford University Press, 1999), p. 54.

[12] Wole Soyinka, *Collected Plays 1* (Oxford: Oxford University Press), 1973, pp. 233-307; for comment see W. Sotto, *The Rounded Rite* (Lund: CWK Gleerup, 1985). Donna Tartt, *The Secret History* (London: Penguin, 1993); for comment see B. Arkins, *Classical and Modern Literature* 15(1995), pp. 281-87.

[13] Colin Teevan, *Euripides – Bacchae* (London: Oberon Books, 2002).

[14] Edith Hall in Teevan (note 13), pp. 9-14.

[15] *ibid.*, p. 10.

[16] *ibid.*, p. 13.

[17] Morwood (note 11), p. 64.

[16] Teevan (note 13), p. 42.

[19] *ibid.*, p. 21

[20] *ibid.*, pp. 67-68.

[21] *ibid.*, p. 70.

[22] Derek Mahon, *The Bacchae* (Oldcastle: Gallery Press, 1991). For *High Time* see F. O'Toole, *Critical Moments*, eds. J. Furey and R. O'Hanlon (Dublin: Carysfort Press, 2003), pp. 29-32.

[23] Friedrich Nietzsche, *The Birth of Tragedy*. Cited by Mahon, p. 9.

[24] E.R. Dodds, *The Greeks and the Irrational* (Berkeley: University of California Press, 1951).

[25] Louis MacNeice, *The Poetry of W.B. Yeats* (London: Faber & Faber, 1979), p. 123.

[26] Derek Mahon, *Collected Poems* (Oldcastle: Gallery Press, 1999), p. 242.

[27] Mahon (note 22), pp. 13-15.

[28] *ibid.*, p. 62; cf. p. 41.

[29] *ibid.*, p. 12; p. 16; p. 18; p. 49; p.14.

[30] Morwood (note 11), p. 76.

[31] Mahon (note 22), p. 49.

[32] *ibid.*, p. 12; p. 13.

[33] *ibid.*, p. 17; p. 37.

[34] *ibid.*, p. 22; R. Kitzinger, quoted back cover of Mahon (note 22).

[35] For Shaw and the Classics see M. von Albrecht, *Classical and Modern Literature* 8(1987), pp. 33-46; 8(1988), pp. 105-14. For *Major Barbara* see, e.g., M.M. Morgan, *The Shavian Playground* (London: Methuen, 1974), pp. 134-57; A.M. Gibbs, *The Art and Mind of Shaw* (London: Macmillan, 1983), pp. 153-67; N. Crane, *Bernard Shaw – A Critical View* (London: Macmillan, 1984), pp. 84-100.

[36] Shaw, quoted in Macintosh (note 39), p. 76.

[37] Bernard Shaw, *Major Barbara* (London: Penguin, n.d.), pp. 109-10.

[38] *ibid.*, p. 95; pp. 93-4; pp. 107-08; p. 115.

[39] S.P. Albert, *Educational Theatre Journal* 20, 2(1968), pp. 123-40; F. Macintosh, *Classics Ireland* 5(1998), pp. 64-84.

[40] A further link to Euripides lies in the fact that Cusins is a foundling like Ion in *Ion*; cf. Morgan (note 35), p. 152.

[41] Shaw (note 37), p. 15; p. 143.

[42] Translation by D. Lee.

[43] Shaw (note 37), p. 147.

[44] D. Kiberd, *Inventing Ireland* (London: Jonathan Cape, 1995), p. 61.

[45] Shaw (note 37), p. 58; cf. p. 59; p. 116.

9 | Euripides' *Trojan Women* and *Hecuba*

1

Euripides' tragedy *The Trojan Women*,[1] which was produced in Athens in 415 BC and won second prize, deals with the total destruction of the Trojan civilization by the Greeks at the end of the Trojan War.[2] This scenario is presented by Euripides not so much as narrative as a very poignant oratorio (as with the initial monody of Hecuba that expresses extreme suffering). In Greek mythology, the war between the Greeks and the Trojans, which lasted for ten years, was the paradigmatic war that put all others in the shade, while in Greek and Roman warfare in general the sack of a city was a disastrous, climactic event. So In *The Trojan Women*, in material terms, the walls of Troy, essential to the city (*polis*), together with its towers, are in ruins; in cultural terms, the temples and altars of the gods have also vanished. The matter can be summed up in Hecuba's assertion: 'Troy, unhappy Troy, you no longer exist'.[3]

But in *The Trojan Women*, the main part of Troy's disaster lies in having the royal women allotted as sexual slaves to various Greek leaders, leading to the fragmentation of the royal house. Hecuba, the Trojan queen who dominates the action of the play, goes to the hated Odysseus; her daughter the prophetess Cassandra is given to the Greek commander-in-chief Agamemnon; Andromache, the wife of the Trojan warrior Hector is assigned to Neoptolemus, son of the Greek warrior Achilles (Since these Greek leaders live respectively in Ithaca, Argos, and Thessaly, Athens is desired by the Trojan women, but never reached). Furthermore, it is revealed that Hecuba's other daughter Polyxena has already been sacrificed on the tomb of Achilles in a bloody and brutal parody of a marriage ceremony; and Astyanax, the son of Hector and Andromache, is also killed in order to ensure that the Trojan royal line is totally wiped out (Seneca's tragedy *The Trojan Women* enacts *both* those events). As all this progresses, the Greek herald Talthybius provides a link between sections of the play, sympathetic to the Trojans, but dashing any hopes they may have.4

But there is some recompense for the Trojans. Because of Greek desecration of her altar (*hubris*), the goddess Athene joins forces with the god Poseidon to ensure that the Greek journey home is very difficult. In a long scene (lines 294-461) in which she is partly manic, partly controlled, Cassandra elaborates on this: Agamemnon will be murdered on his return by Clytemnestra, and she will in turn be murdered by Orestes; Odysseus is fated to wander for ten years before coming home. So Cassandra, in what might seem a perverse way, can hymn her 'marriage' to Agamemnon. These prophecies of Cassandra obviously relate to the future, but in the present *The Trojan Women* offers another form of recompense to Troy: the Trojan Women *speak*, and in Greek terms at that, because they no longer inhabit the inner space of the house (*oikos*) and have moved into public space; powerless those women may be, but they have retained a capacity for eloquence.

The appearance of Helen5 raises the fundamental *moral* question of who was responsible for the Trojan War. In this contest (*agon*) between Helen and Hecuba, both make use of the techniques of Greek rhetoric to put forward their case (women blame other women), with Helen's egregious efforts to dissolve herself of responsibility for the war strangely suggesting the Sophist Gorgias' *Encomium of Helen* (whose relativism was an important influence on Euripides).

Euripides' *The Trojan Women* has always been viewed as an anti-war play. When it was first performed in 415 BC, the Peloponnesian War between Athens and Sparta had been underway for sixteen years, and it is impossible not to feel that this major, lengthy conflict will have left its mark on *The Trojan Women*.6 More specifically, the events of the previous year 416 BC on the Aegean island of Melos provided a gruesome parallel to the action of *The Trojan Women*. A Doric state which had not been part of the Athenian Empire, which declined to pay tribute to Athens, and which decided to assist Sparta, Melos refused to surrender to Athens. The result was that the island was captured by Athens, its male inhabitants put to death, its women and children sold as slaves.

Scorned for centuries, *The Trojan Women* came into its own again in a twentieth century plagued by vicious wars, and became one of the most frequently performed of Euripides' plays.[7] Indeed modern adaptations of *The Trojan Women* can be seen to fulminate against various contemporary wars: Gilbert Murray's translation was directed against the First World War; Cacoyannis' film (1971) attacked the war in Vietnam; Sartre's *Les Troyennes* (1965) castigated the French war in Algeria; Suzuki's Tokyo production (1974) clearly suggested Hiroshima. No wonder then that Hamilton maintained that *The Trojan Women* is 'a timeless indictment of the horror and futility of all wars'.[8]

2

Irish appropriation of Euripides' *The Trojan Women* takes the form of a version by Brendan Kennelly and a loose adaptation by Aidan Mathews.

Brendan Kennelly's 'version' of *The Trojan Women*[9] keeps the invariant core of Euripides' tragedy, but expands considerably on the original and brings out in a very marked way the resilience of the women of Troy. So this third Athenian play of Kennelly's allows him to continue the interest in women that he had already shown in *Antigone* and *Medea*. Kennelly sees *The Trojan Women* as a play about war and the consequences of war for women: 'The play as I understand it, is, very briefly, about the consequences of war, it's about the men who win and the women who lose.[10] But at the same time, the women of Troy for Kennelly are resilient: 'within that apparent passivity of victims, I increasingly found a strong active, resolute and shrewd note'.[11]

Hence the god Poseidon begins Kennelly's play by asserting that women, for all their parlous state, will come to control things: 'women will rule the world'. In her first speech, Hecuba seems to concur: she certainly hinges on the extreme desolation of Troy, but also envisages fighting back and winning: 'Yet, may not a woman/fight, yes, fight, here and now?/May not a woman win?' Consequently, Hecuba urges the other Trojan women to produce a 'cry', that will change the world. Like the cry that brings down 'God's curse on every rutting man', a man whose sexual domination is seen as functioning through the male gaze: 'A man's eyes can strip me naked in a way.' For Kennelly, Cassandra too is positive, believing that the Trojan women are, despite appearances to the contrary, happier than the Greeks: 'You and I and these women/are happier than the Greeks, our conquerors'. But as the Trojan women are allotted to their Greek leaders, the mood becomes more sombre, so that Hecuba utters the very Greek sentiment 'No human can be happy/this side of the grave';[12] compare Sophocles, *Oedipus at Colonus* 1389: Not to be born is best when all is reckoned in.'[13]

Soon, however, a note of determination returns to the women. While Andromache laments that she is to be possessed by Achilles' son (who murdered her husband Hector), she is convinced that she can somehow rise above all this: 'And yet clearly see/that if my body is a slave/an untouched portion of my mind is free'. In this optimism, Andromache is encouraged by Hecuba: 'He thinks you're his slave;/you know he's yours.'[14]

In the Helen scene, Hecuba is bluntly scathing about what she sees as Helen's exploitation of her sexuality – 'I see a cunt. I see an evil cunt' – and of her avarice: 'I see a greedy, scheming bitch'. But Hecuba can be equally cynical herself in a piece not found in Euripides: 'Pick one, Helen. Pick a man. Fuck him. Let him die. / Stick him in a grave, cold, deep, far from the sun. / And remember always – take care of number one.'[15]

Hecuba is even more eloquent in a long speech towards the end of Kennelly's play, powerfully affirming her human identity through the anaphora of 'I am not':[16]

> I am Hecuba, Hecuba, nobody but Hecuba,
> I am not a prize, I am not a slave, not a slave
> To anyone living or dead,
> I am not a decoration or an ornament,
> I am not a bit of scandal or a piece of gossip
> I am not something to be pointed at,
> I am not something to be used at someone's beck and call,
> I am not a thing, I am not a fuck ...

And yet Hecuba must cross the Aegean to Greece, a crossing stressed by the sea imagery that is pervasive in Kennelly (as in Euripides): 'God's overwhelming waves are drowning me!' Indeed Hecuba compares herself to the sea: 'A wave of the sea! / Natural and fearless'. These waves are cosmic, innumerable, knowledgeable, subject to pleasure and pain, symbolic of Hecuba's ambivalent position, and her final exultation:

> The waves roar and moan in pain.
> The waves laugh happily.
> The waves are slaves.

The waves are free.
The war is over. The war begins – for me![17]

3

Aidan Mathew's loose adaptation of Euripides' *The Trojan Women* called *Trojans*[18] is set (like Brecht's *Antigone*) in Berlin in 1945 at the end of World War II. In a preliminary note to his play, Mathews observes that Euripides' tragedy of 415 BC rendered the Peloponnesian War in general and the matter of Melos in particular problematical: 'So legend countermanded propaganda, myth critiqued atrocity, and pre-history lit up history itself, for nothing is more topical than antiquity'. Equally well, Euripides casts light on our own contemporary world: Europe 'copies the themes and the types of conflict that Euripides wrote about as an eye-witness to the Peloponnesian war'. This is specially true of modern democracy's appeasement of Nazi Germany: 'our supremacist Anglo-American continues to congratulate itself on a democratic mystique that did little to prevent the birth of Nazism in the nineteen thirties',[19] Mathews's play, then, stresses the interaction of ancient and modern in the context of a prevailing desolation; as Athena says, 'The smell of the dead hangs over everything'.[20]

Mathews's play is resolutely modern in most respects. While the characters retain their Greek names, and their clever talk recalls Euripidean rhetoric (especially the Helen episode), they belong to the period of World War II: Hecuba is the wife of a Wehrmacht officer; Andromache is a war widow of the Reich; Helen is a general secretary, and the chorus secretaries of the Reich Chancellery; Poseidon and Athena (who play a greater role than in Euripides) are respectively a crippled submarine veteran and a Weimar demi-mondaine. In a reversal of Greek practice, all the actors are female.

A series of links between Germany and Greece point up not merely the Nazi delusion that the Reich is akin to Classical Greece (Hitler ordered excavations in Olympia to discover true Aryans!), but also the essential fragility of Greek and of modern European culture.

To begin with, the concept of Greek theatre is itself subject to loss and parody. The set is certainly that of 'A SMALL GREEK THEATRE', and the situation described by Poseidon (a submarine veteran) is that of a 'Greek tragedy'. But the theatre has 'RUINED TERRACES'; the demi-mondaine Athena refers to 'the seventy-seven lost plays of Sophocles' and the 'eighty-five missing works of

Euripides'; and the current Greek tragedy will be followed by a satyr play of 'Turkish delights' in the shape of creature comforts.[21]

Also undercut is the official German line that there are close links between Greece and Nazi Germany as experienced by the Establishment and by ordinary people. We learnt that Government buildings have 'GRAECO-ROMAN COLUMNS' and that Greta 'kept a miniature model of the Parthenon on her mantelpiece'. But there is a mockery of Austrian psychiatrists 'who think that ancient Greece is the holy land', and Woman 3 notes that her husband 'went down... like Icarus'. Then Lessing held that Greek torsos in Munich were 'complete', when in fact they were without limbs. And while Talthybius (a British officer) talks of 'the Graeco-German and the Germano-Greek, Poseidon believes that the Greek for Germany is 'Shit and scheisse', and the *lingua franca* for the British and the Russians turns out not to be Greek, but Latin.[22]

Such fragility in culture paves the way for Mathews's portrait of the desolation caused by war, which is presented with the edge of modern cynicism. In general, nobody here is innocent; all are tainted by war and by human vulnerability. Hence the sexual submission of the Trojan women to the Greeks is transformed into the sexual desire both of the Allies and the Nazis. Hence the murder of Hector's son Astyanax is changed into the death of a very young boy from illness in hospital.

Mathews's characters, divine and human, deal in loss and forms of loss caused by evil during the Nazi era of 'bread and circuses'. Poseidon, who asserts that 'I don't believe in anything', believes that 'Europe is over'. For Athena, Berlin is not the imperial city of Rome, but ruined Troy – 'We thought we were building Rome. We were building Troy' – and she must therefore parody Sophocles' Ode to Man: 'for wonders are many and none is more wonderful than them'. Transformed into a Roman Catholic nun, Cassandra asserts that her community is to be found 'On the altarlist of the dead and the files of the Gestapo'; notes that the hearts of German women married to Nazis were somehow removed by their victims; and believes that all is presided over 'by the ravenous jaws/Of those who keep their mouths shut on the commuter trains'.[23]

4

Euripides' tragedy *Hecuba*[24] (mid 420s BC) shows that the story of the Trojan queen Hecuba after the fall of Troy is rich in dramatic possibilities: in this play, she may enjoy a central role for the first time. As so often, Euripides focuses on the plight of women, on Hecuba who is 'the greatest sufferer among mortals' (line 721). But the tragedy *Hecuba* shows that Hecuba is capable of devastating revenge, what Bacon calls 'a kind of wild justice'. Indeed after Erasmus' translation of *Hecuba* into Latin (1503), it became the archetypal example of the revenge tragedy that was so popular in the Renaissance, notably in England between 1588 and 1642. So the intense way in which Hecuba's suffering is experienced leads to Hamlet's famous question to the Player 'What's Hecuba to him, or he to Hecuba/That he should weep for her?'[25]

As the Greek fleet is delayed from sailing home from Troy by contrary winds, Hecuba's daughter Polyxena must be sacrificed to the ghost of Achilles, a death that will ensure that no more warriors will be born to fight for Troy. Hecuba seeks to prevent Odysseus, whose life she had saved, from leading Polyxena away, but the Trojan princess in any case prefers death to slavery. When Hecuba is getting ready to bury Polyxena, a further disaster occurs involving her youngest son Polydorus who has been sent for safety to Polymestor ('Much-planning'), the king of the Thracians Chersonese, with part of the treasure of Troy. In Greek literature, Thracians are often portrayed as savage, greedy and cowardly: so here Polymestor wants the treasure for himself, murders Polydorus – the killing of a guest is horrific in Greek thought – throws his body into the sea, and so fails to bury him (a terrible fate for the Greeks, as we see in *Antigone*).

The body of Polydorus is washed up and brought to Hecuba, who tries without success to persuade the Greek leader Agamemnon to exact vengeance. Hecuba then acts on her own, in accordance with the Greek principle that you do evil to your enemies: she lures Polymestor and his sons into her tent, where her women put out the Thracian's eyes (a punishment for acts of betrayal), and kill the sons. In the face of the breakdown of the city (*polis*) of Troy, no other option is possible, Hecuba being a hero-avenger, not a villain-revenger. But the fate of Hecuba is ambivalent: while Polymestor is to be placed on a deserted island, Hecuba is to be transformed into a dog, with the site of her tomb marked by the name Cynossema, 'Dog's tomb'.

5

Frank McGuinness's 'version of Euripides' *Hecuba* premiered at the Donmar Warehouse in London in September 2004.[26] Just as Yeats for his versions of *King Oedipus at Colonus* worked from the prose translation of Jebb, so McGuinness worked 'from a literal translation' by Fionnuala Murphy. McGuinness sticks closely to the plot line of *Hecuba*, stressing the suffering Hecuba experiences after the deaths of Polyxena and Polydorus, and her violent revenge on Polymestor. But McGuinness introduces a major stylistic innovation by his use for much of the play of a very short verse line.

In the Episodes of Greek tragedy, the iambic trimeter metre normally results in a line of 12 syllables, but McGuinness often reduces the number of syllables in a drastic way that makes for a lucid, lyrical quality. So in the first part of *Hecuba's* opening statement by the Ghost of Polydorus (lines 1-2), McGuinness uses lines of five, four and even three syllables:[27]

> I am Polydorus, son of Hecuba.
> Priam is my father.
> I am dead.
> I come from that darkness –
> The abyss, the gates of goddess hell.
> Son of Hecuba,
> Priam is my father –
> He sent me from Troy
> Besieged by the Greeks;
> Fearing the fall of Troy,
> He secreted me
> Away from Thrace,
> To the home of his friend,
> Polymestor, old friend,
> Who ploughs that fertile land,
> Who rules its horsemen.
> My father hid with me
> A hoard of gold
> Should the wall of Troy fall
> His children would not want.

Later in the play when Hecuba has exacted revenge on Polymestor and the two talk to each other in the one-line exchanges of stichomythia, McGuinness uses a very short line in order to present the issue in a most elemental way (lines 1255-61):[28]

> Polymestor: I suffer for my children –
> I suffer to my eyes.
> Hecuba: You feel pain –
> What of it?
> Do I not feel pain?
> Pain for my son?
> Polymestor: Woman, you take pleasure
> As you punish.

Hecuba: I take pleasure
In revenge, my revenge.
Polymestor: It won't last long.
Wait for the wet sea.
Hecuba: To carry me
To the wilds of Greece?
Polymestor: No – the sea will swallow you.
You will fall from the head of a mast.

But McGuinness varies his style in *Hecuba* by sometimes employing a long line. So in Hecuba's lengthy address to Agamemnon, her plea for justice is enhanced by the long line which, while lucid, is more substantial than the short lines found elsewhere in the play (lines 798-809):[29]

I stand here a slave, I may have no strength,
But the gods are strong – so too is the law.
It rules over all, mortal, immortal.
Spit on the law, murder friends, ransack holy planes,
And if you pay no penalty nor punishment –
There is no justice among men – no justice.
But if you judge there to be acts of shame,
Respect me, pity me, observe what I suffer.
I was once sovereign, now I am a slave.
Blessed with children then, now I lose children.
I ruled a city – that city is no more.

---

[1] For *The Trojan Women* see K.H. Lee, *Euripides – Troades* (London: Oxford University Press, 1976); S.A. Barlow, *Euripides – Trojan Women* (Warminster: Aris & Phillips, 1986); N.T. Croally, *Euripides – Polemic – The Trojan Women and the Function of Tragedy* (Cambridge: Cambridge University Press, 1994).

[2] A Poole, *Arion* 3(1976), pp. 257-87.

[3] J. Morwood, *Euripides – The Trojan Women and Other Plays* (Oxford: Oxford University Press, 2000), p. 43.

[4] K. Gilmartin, *American Journal of Philology* 91(1970), pp. 213-22.

[5] M. Lloyd, *Classical Quarterly* 34(1984), pp. 303-13.

[6] Croally (note 1), pp. 231-34.

[7] F. Macintosh in *The Cambridge Companion to Greek Tragedy* ed. P.E. Easterling (Cambridge: Cambridge University Press, 1997), pp. 284-323.

[8] Edith Hamilton, quoted in M. McDonald, *Ancient Sun, Modern Light: Greek Drama on the Modern Stage* (New York: Columbia University Press, 1992), p. 35.

[9] Brendan Kennelly, *Euripides' The Trojan Women* (Newcastle-upon-Tyne: Bloodaxe, 1993). For comment see K. McCracken in *Dark Fathers into Light: Brendan Kennelly*, ed. R. Pine (Newcastle-upon-

Tyne: Bloodaxe, 1994), pp. 139-47; M. Lloyd, *Classics Ireland* 1(1994), pp. 54-60.

[10] Kennelly, quoted in McCracken (note 9), p. 139.

[11] Kennelly (note 9), p. 5.

[12] *ibid.*, p. 7; pp. 13-14; p. 14; p. 18; p. 13; p. 24; p. 32.

[13] R. Fagles, *Sophocles – The Three Theban Plays* (Harmondsworth: Penguin, 1984), p. 358.

[14] Kennelly, (note 9), pp. 39-40; p. 41.

[15] *ibid.*, p. 59; p. 58.

[16] *ibid.*, pp. 73-74.

[17] *ibid.*, p. 40; p. 79.

[18] I am grateful to Mr. Mathews for providing me with the typescript of *Trojans*.

[19] Mathews (note 18), p. 2.

[20] *ibid.*, p. 11.

[21] *ibid.*, p. 4; p. 18; p. 40.

[22] *ibid.*, p. 4; p. 8; p. 22; p. 13; p. 14; p. 42; p. 43.

[23] *ibid.*, p. 17; p. 5; p. 7; p. 13; pp. 18-19; p. 21.

[24] For *Hecuba* see M. Nussbaum, *The Fragility of Goodness* (Cambridge: Cambridge University Press, 1986), pp. 397-422; C. Collard, *Euripides' Hecuba* (Warminster: Aris & Phillips, 1991); J. Mossman, *Wild Justice: A Study of Euripides' Hecuba* (Oxford: Oxford University Press, 1995).

[25] Shakespeare, *Hamlet*, Act 2, Scene 2, lines 553-54.

[26] Frank McGuinness, *Euripides' Hecuba* (London: Faber & Faber, 2004).

[27] *ibid.*, p. 3.

[28] *ibid.*, p. 60.

[29] *ibid.*, p. 38.

10 | Euripides' *Hippolytus*

1

The plot of Euripides' *Hippolytus*,[1] which was produced in 428 BC and won first prize, involves the sexual love of Phaedra, wife of Theseus, king of Athens, for the stepson Hippolytus (the son of Theseus by the Amazon queen Hippolyte). Similar stories of the passion of an older woman for a younger man are found in the Old Testament account of Potiphar's wife, and in Euripides' lost play *Stheneboea*. This motif of the love of a stepmother for a stepson will have had a special resonance in Greek society, where many women died in childbirth and their husbands remarried.

In *Hippolytus*, we encounter two of the powers who control the universe, Aphrodite and Artemis. Both Phaedra and Hippolytus are seen to be in breach of what is required by Aphrodite, goddess of love and of sexuality. Phaedra comes from a sexually deviant background because she is the daughter of Pasiphae who slept with a bull and bore the Minotaur; because she is the sister of Ariadne who abandoned the god Dionysus and went off with Theseus; and because she is the granddaughter of Aerape who slept with her husband's brother. Accordingly, Phaedra falls in love with Hippolytus in a quasi-incestuous relationship. Phaedra recognizes her guilt intermittently – she calls it *hamartia* (323) – eloquently deplores it, and resolves to die.

When Phaedra's passion is discovered by the Nurse (a stock character) and related to Hippolytus, he is horrified; discovered and rejected, Phaedra hangs herself, the preferred mode of suicide for women in tragedy. But Phaedra has written a letter to her husband Theseus denouncing Hippolytus as her seducer. Outraged, Theseus invokes the curse of his father the sea-god Poseidon upon

Hippolytus and also decides to banish him. Thus the contest (*agon*) between Theseus and Hippolytus can deal with the topic of exile. As Hippolytus drives away from the palace, the curse is fulfilled: a monstrous bull sent by Poseidon from the malevolent sea ensures that he is thrown from his chariot and severely injured. This bull is clearly a sexual symbol, representing Phaedra's abnormal passion and underlining Hippolytus' excessive rejection of sexuality. Artemis then appears as a *deus ex machina* and tells Theseus of the innocence of the dying Hippolytus, who absolves his suffering father of guilt. Thus by the end of *Hippolytus*, the characters achieve the knowledge[2] that had eluded them during the course of the action: 'The desire for clear knowledge or true witness voiced by the Chorus, Nurse, Phaedra, Theseus, Hippolytus leads to naught'.[3] So *Hippolytus*, like *King Oedipus*, is, *inter alia*, a play about *knowledge*.

If Phaedra is guilty, so too is Hippolytus. Honoured in cult and legend in Troezen, Hippolytus refuses to pay homage to Aphrodite, goddess of sexuality, and instead worships the virgin goddess Artemis in a way that allows him to claim for himself, in an extraordinary way, *moral* purity.[4] Artemis is a goddess of the wilderness and of the hunt, she is a virgin, she is goddess of childbirth. What unites these three facts is the theme of *separation*:[5] as a virgin goddess, Artemis keeps men and women apart; as goddess of childbirth, she supervises an experience that only women can have; and as goddess of the wilderness and the hunt, she separates civilization and wild nature. Artemis is therefore the goddess of sexual otherness, just as Aphrodite is the goddess of sexual coming together. By his fanatical devotion to Artemis and rejection of sex, Hippolytus cuts himself off from normal human life, separates himself from other men, seeks to become what Wordsworth calls 'Nature's priest'. Indeed Hippolytus launches into a ferocious tirade against the whole female sex in the presence of Phaedra, asserting that in an ideal world there would be no women and no sex.

The action of *Hippolytus* seems to be determined by the goddess Aphrodite: 'In no other Greek tragedy is the predetermination of human action by an external power made so emphatically clear'.[6] Aphrodite is a goddess born from the sea, and, like it, vast, powerful, inscrutable; she will destroy Hippolytus, the devotee of Artemis, virgin goddess of pure streams.[7] But Aphrodite's telling of events in the Prologue cancels Euripides' innovation in

Hippolytus:[8] in the familiar form of the legend, Phaedra, when rejected by Hippolytus, accused him of rape to Theseus, face-to-face, with the result that Hippolytus is cursed and dies, and that Phaedra then commits suicide; but in Euripides, Phaedra commits suicide first to save her honour and accuses Hippolytus to Theseus in a letter. Furthermore, Euripides engineers an ironic juxtaposition, in which the human characters are involved in a complicated *series of choices* involving speech and silence that establish *Hippolytus* as a play about knowledge: Phaedra says she will not reveal her love for Hippolytus, and then talks about it to the Chorus; the Nurse urges Phaedra to reveal her love, regrets this, and then urges Phaedra to further speech; Hippolytus decides to tell Theseus, but then changes his mind.

2

Irish appropriation of Euripides' *Hippolytus* is found in Brian Friel's play *Living Quarters* (1977) and Ulick O'Connor's *The Oval Machine*.[9]

Friel's *Living Quarters*[10] ('a seriously neglected work')[11] is stated by the author to be 'after Hippolytus' and the basic plot line is clearly Euripidean, but the play draws on other dramatic resources besides Euripides: the family setting is from Chekhov; the independence of the characters suggests Pirandello; and the way the characters re-enact events recalls Yeats's concept of the dreaming back.

The family in question in *Living Quarters* is that of Commandant Frank Butler, who has had a distinguished career in the Irish army and whose recent exploits while serving abroad with the United Nations result in a major local celebration in Ballybeg. Like Theseus, Butler is a man of action, a military figure who is absent from home at the crucial time; that is when, after the death of his first wife, he has married the much younger Anna, but has spent little time with her. Butler contrasts with his weak son Ben, who is unable to face up to adult life and enjoys a kind of permanent adolescence; his sister Miriam says 'Ben is a wastrel – a spoiled mother's boy'.[12] Ben therefore mirrors the inability of Hippolytus to face up to the requirements of adult sexuality, and both young men have a poor relationship with their father.

As Phaedra from Athens lives in exile in Troezen, so Anna must live, bored and neglected, in deepest Donegal. In the absence of her husband Frank she has an abortive affair with her step-son Ben. So whereas in Euripides Phaedra's advance are rejected by Hippolytus, in Friel the relationship between Anna and Ben is consummated. Just as in *Hippolytus* the issue of speech or silence is permanent, so in *Living Quarters* much hinges on whether Anna or Ben are to reveal the truth of their relationship: Anna wishes to do so, Ben does not. Eventually Anna speaks the truth to Frank and others in a moment of recognition (*anagnorisis*):[13]

> We had an affair! We were lovers, Ben and I! And everybody in the camp knows! Everybody in Ballybeg knows! Everybody except the Butlers! That's what I'm telling you! We had an affair!

The result of this revelation is devastating and radically alters Euripides. Instead of Phaedra killing herself, it is Frank Butler, the Theseus figure, who commits suicide (though it should be noted that at *Hippolytus* 836-38 Theseus wishes to die after Phaedra's suicide). Just as in Euripides it is the spite of the gods that attacks Phaedra, so in Friel Frank Butler feels hard done by: 'I wish to say that I consider I have been treated unfairly'.[14] Indeed Butler is like another figure from Athenian tragedy, Agamemnon, who also dies when he hoped to enjoy a happy homecoming. The fate of Anna and of Ben is also different from that of Phaedra and Hippolytus who die: Anna carves out a new life for herself in America, and Ben continues his aimless life: 'He has been jailed twice for drunk and disorderly behaviour'.[15]

Whereas in Athenian tragedy, the audience is aware of the basic plot line, but the characters are not, in *Living Quarters* the characters are privy to their own destiny, but the audience is not. Presiding over the reenactment of events in the dysfunctional family of the Butlers is the personage known as Sir. Sir is described as 'Always in full control of the situation, of the other characters, of himself'; he therefore resembles Aphrodite in *Hippolytus* and, like her, speaks the Prologue. Sir is also an omniscient narrator, 'the ultimate arbiter, the powerful and impartial referee, the final adjudicator'.[16] Such knowledge distinguishes Sir from a Greek Chorus, but he resembles the Chorus in being present for all of the action. That action is preordained, since, as in a famous passage by Anouilh, the plot here is inevitable, 'a trap waiting to spring',[17] and represents the triumph of Greek fate over Christian free will.

3

Ulick O'Connor's verse play *The Oval Machine*[18] also transposes Euripides' *Hippolytus* to the modern world, and, in particular, to the game of rugby; as he states in a Note, 'The characters in this play have a relationship with those in Euripides' *Hippolytus*', and, as he writes in the Prologue, 'The condition of mankind is constant'.[19] So the Theseus figure is Bill McGinley, an Irish millionaire in his fifties; the Phaedra figure is Stephanie, his second wife who is much younger (Maureen, his first wife, died); and the Hippolytus figure is Kevin McGinley, Stephanie's step-son. O'Connor's play begins with a Prologue that is spoken by a Chorus and that deals with Aphrodite, the goddess of love, with Artemis, goddess of the hunt, and with the basic plot line of the ancient and the modern story. Whether or not Aphrodite is divine she is certainly a 'force' who presides over power, lust, 'perhaps even love', and who can be resisted by 'very few'. But Aphrodite is tricky: 'Exciting for a while, but ultimately disastrous'.[20] At the same time, Artemis is a 'protector of nature who has as 'her entourage a fleet of athletes', young men who sacrifice 'ambition, lust, and getting on'; even now, 'I say that such there are indeed.'[21]

Bill McGinley was 'the greatest footballer of his time', 'our ideal and our perfect man', but now is devoted to dodgy business deals, a 'voluptuous delight in absolute power',[22] and an obsession with the rugby team he supports, Belmont, winning in an upcoming final game. McGinley's wife Stephanie is disillusioned with all this: 'I married the hero of my youth and now I find he has feet of clay.'[23] But she recognized the 'natural decency' in her step-son Kevin, who dislikes the rougher side of rugby training, violent play, and his father's imperative to win at all costs. Indeed Kevin's devotion to a pure version of rugby mirrors Hippolytus' to the hunt of Artemis: 'I play rugby because I find a joy/In it I can find nowhere else'.[24] Like Hippolytus, Kevin is wholly devoted to his game: 'Sport is always part of my life/And it would not be that/If I didn't get a certain ecstasy from it'. But this ecstasy does not blind Kevin to violent play and the injuries that result from it, and he threatens to pull out of the final if Steve Kidd, the epitomy of that aggressive play, plays in it; as the Chorus says, 'Twice blessed is the dreamer.'[25]

Stephanie is attuned to Kevin's feminine side, as when she finds him reading a Shakespeare play, but she is also aware of Kevin as a man who is 'like a Greek god'. Stephanie finds in Kevin what she once saw in Bill, and she suggests that she could, uniquely, be both lover and mother to him:[26]

> Can I not be a woman to you now
> One whom you will take in your arms.

Become your lover and remain
Something of the mother you never knew.

Stephanie's love is not all one-sided, since Kevin has sexual
fantasies about her. Through the Phaedra figure, Stephanie,
McGinley senses that there is a relationship between Kevin and
Stephanie, accosts Kevin, and, like Hippolytus in Euripides,
fulminates against women.

The climax of *The Oval Machine* comes with the rugby final that
Kevin's team wins, but in which one of Kevin's fellow players is
seriously injured. Unlike Hippolytus, Kevin does not die, but he is
permanently estranged from his father and from rugby. As in
Euripides, the Phaedra figure Stephanie dies, but we do not know
how: 'Stephanie is dead/Whether by accident or design/You shall
not know'. And as in *Hippolytus*, Fate in the form of the Machine
dominates: 'IT IS OBVIOUS THAT MCGINLEY IS NOW IN THE
GRIP OF THE MACHINE FROM WHICH HE CANNOT ESCAPE.'[27]

---

[1] For Euripides' *Hippolytus* see *Euripides' Hippolytus*, ed. W.S. Barrett
(Oxford: Oxford University Press, 1964); M.R. Halleran, *Hippolytus*
(Warminster: Aris & Phillips, 1995); C. Luschnig, *Time Holds the
Mirror: A Study of Knowledge in Euripides' Hippolytus* (Leiden: Brill,
1988).

[2] For knowledge see Luschnig (note 1).

[3] Luschnig (note 1), p. 87.

[4] C.P. Segal, *Hermes* 98(1970), pp. 278-80.

[5] W. Sale, *Existentialism and Euripides* (Berwick: Aureal Publications,
1977), pp. 39-53.

[6] B.M.W. Knox in *Euripides*, ed. E. Segal (Englewood Cliffs, N.J.: Prentice-
Hall, 1968), p. 91.

[7] C.P. Segal, *HSCP* 70(1965), pp. 117-69.

[8] Barrett (note 1), *ad* 41-50.

[9] A third play that is supposedly derived from Euripides' *Hippolytus* is
Autumn Fire by T.C. Murray (text in *Selected Plays of T.C. Murray*, ed.
R.A. Cave (Gerrards Cross/Washington D.C.: Colin Smythe, 1998), pp.
119-77); for this view see R.A. Cave in *Amid Our Troubles – Irish
Versions of Greek Tragedy*, eds. M. McDonald and J.M. Walton
(London: Methuen, 2002), pp. 110-27. But the only link between
Autumn Fire and *Hippolytus* is the tentative relationship between
Owen Keegan's second wife Nance Desmond and his son Michael (a
relationship not pursued by the Phaedra figure, Nance, but by the
Hippolytus figure Michael). This relationship, by itself, cannot mean
that *Autumn Fire* is based on *Hippolytus*.

[10] Brian Friel, *Selected Plays* (London: Faber & Faber, 1984), pp. 171-246.
For comment see A. Peacock in *The Achievement of Brian Friel*, ed. A.
Peacock (Gerrards Cross: Colin Smythe, 1993), pp. 113-20; T. Kilroy,
ibid., pp. 93-97; M. Lloyd, *Irish University Review* 30(2000), pp. 244-

53; R. O'Hanlon in *Theatre Stuff*, ed. E. Jordan (Dublin: Carysfort Press, 2000), pp. 107-21; R.A. Cave in *Amid Our Troubles* (note 9), pp. 101-10.

[11] Kilroy (note 10), p. 97.

[12] Friel (note 10), p. 187.

[13] *ibid.*, p. 238.

[14] *ibid.*, p. 240.

[15] *ibid.*, p. 245.

[16] *ibid.*, p. 175; pp. 177-78.

[17] *ibid.*, p. 177.

[18] I am grateful to Dr Redmond O'Hanlon of University College, Dublin for providing me with a typescript of *The Oval Theatre* by Ulick O'Connor. References below are to the pages of this typescript.

[19] O'Connor (note 18), p. 4.

[20] *ibid.*

[21] *ibid.*, p. 5.

[22] *ibid.*, p. 6.

[23] *ibid.*, p. 8.

[24] *ibid.*, p. 9; p. 11.

[25] *ibid.*, p. 12; p. 18.

[26] *ibid.*, p. 26;p. 29.

[27] *ibid.*, p. 43.

11 | Euripides' *Iphigenia in Aulis*

1

Euripides' late tragedy *Iphigenia in Aulis*[1] was produced post-humously in about 405 BC and contains several spurious passages, notably a happy ending.[2] *Iphigenia in Aulis* deals with the sacrifice of his daughter Iphigenia (which means nobly born) by the Greek leader Agamemnon which is necessary to allow the becalmed Greek fleet sail to Troy; according to the seer Calchas, the goddess Artemis (who rules Aulis in Boeotia) requires this sacrifice for which no reason is given, The dilemma for Agamemnon, the central *aporia* of the play, was that he was faced with an impossible choice between killing his daughter and abandoning the Greek expedition to Troy (the spectators know, of course, that the war against Troy will take place). From Iphigenia's point of view, she finds herself among a group of military men who are lying, shameless, self-centred, full of bluster, and with a selective memory.

Forced to choose either personal happiness or military power, Agamemnon vacillates. First, he rejects the idea of killing Iphigenia. Then he changes his mind and sends for Iphigenia on the pretext that she is to marry Achilles (who knows nothing of this); as he says, in reality she will marry death: 'Hades, it seems, will soon marry her.'[3] But Agamemnon cancels the summons of Iphigenia; his brother Menelaus, however, intercepts this second message. This theme of vacillation continues apace. When Clytemnestra and her daughter Iphigenia arrive in Aulis, Menelaus changes his mind and offers to give up the Greek expedition. But Agamemnon has also changed his mind (again), because he is afraid of the anger of the army if he abandons the expedition to Troy. So Iphigenia must be killed, and Clytemnestra points out that this is not the first time

Agamemnon has killed a child of hers: he murdered her first husband Tantalus and her baby by him (this is the invention of Euripides). Discovering that he has been used to deceive Iphigenia, Achilles tries to save her.

Iphigenia first tries to save herself, but then changes *her* mind and acquiesces to her fate, so that she appears to reject being an object of pity in order to become a heroic martyr. Aristotle famously objected to this as being inconsistent: 'An example of inconsistency is the *Iphigenia in Aulis*: when she pleads for her life to be spared she is not at all like her later self'.[4] But here what operates is *Realpolitik*. Iphigenia is *forced* to accept her death, although she then makes the best of it by ironically stating that she is giving her body for Greece.[5] But we may also feel that Iphigenia and the other characters as depicted by Euripides possess all-too-human characteristics that do not belong in the mythical tradition in which they find themselves. So when Iphigenia is first a suppliant for her life and then a person willing to die as the heroic tradition demands, 'It is possible that the purpose of the two Iphigenias is to compel the spectators to notice the anomaly in the tradition and in the behaviour it suggests is proper'.[6]

In the interpolated happy ending of *Iphigenia in Aulis*, Iphigenia mysteriously disappears at the moment she is to be killed, and a deer is substituted as victim; she will live among the gods.

While *Iphigenia in Aulis* is not as well known as some other plays of Euripides, a number of significant translations and adaptations of it have been made. It was the first Greek tragedy to be translated into English, by Lady Jane Lumley in the 1550s.[7] Racine's influential version *Iphigenie en Aulide* came in 1674, and a Modern French version *Les Atrides* by Ariane Mnouchkine in 1990. Cacoyannis made a very successful film version in 1977.[8]

2

Colin Teevan's *Iph...*, described as 'after Euripides' *Iphigenia in Aulis*', is a version of that play which premiered at the Lyric Theatre in Belfast in March 1999.[9] Conscious of the interpolations in *Iphigenia in Aulis*, Teevan 'stripped away the additions and accretions and distortions, translated that which remains';[10] hence the happy ending goes. At the same time, Teevan invents a new beginning and a new ending to *Iph...* that flesh out the myth of Troy. At the beginning of the play, an Old Man from Aeschylus' tragedy *Agamemnon* (identified with the Old Man of *Iphigenia in*

Aulis) notes the fall of Troy, while at the end of the play Klytaimnestra kills Agamemnon on his return from that city.

Central to *Iphigenia in Aulis* for Teevan are 'Agamemnon's dilemma, Klytaimnestra's fierce defence of her child, Iphigenia's initial refusal to sacrifice herself for Greece and her ultimate acceptance'. Teevan sees Agamemnon's dilemma in which he must either sacrifice his daughter Iphigenia or give up the Greek expedition to Troy as 'the debate between the *koinos* and the *idios* – the community and the self'. In regard to Iphigenia's inconsistency, Teevan holds that 'her turn around in thinking is not inconsistent with the character of an adolescent girl who is under an enormous amount of moral duress to "do the right thing"'.[11]

In his version of *Iphigenia in Aulis*, Teevan aims at producing 'a tight muscular idiom like the original Greek', and 'as Anglo-Saxon a register as was feasible'[12] (this is like the register of Hopkins' poems).[13] Hence Klytaimnestra asks 'Must Iphgeneia foot the bill for my sister's sluttery?' and Menelaus upbraids his brother Agamemnon:[14]

> So it's no wonder then
> That when the Greeks came here to Aulis,
> Your command began to crumble.
> The gods stilled the western winds;
> The warmen, restless, itching for a fight,
> Began to voice their discontent.
> Some demanded you disband the fleet.
> How downjawed you appeared;
> What point in all that politicking
> If you could not lead our strong prowed ships or Troy?
> You asked me, your brother, what to do,
> How might you retrieve authority.
> I told you what Kalchas had divined;
> That you must sacrifice to Artemis.
> You were relieved.
> And without any pressure or persuasion
> You commanded Klytaimnestra
> Send your eldest daughter,
> Here to marry Achilleus.
> The heavens heard these things.
> Now, you have aboutfaced once again.

Teevan takes considerable liberties with the Chorus, believing that it must exhibit 'a contemporary sensibility' and 'be set on a journey towards a deeper understanding of themselves'.[15] Hence exchanges of this type:[16]

CHORUS MEMBER: Penis, like all men, could not help himself –
CHORUS MEMBER: When it came to himself helping himself.
CHORUS MEMBER:Aphrodite brought him to her bed.
CHORUS MEMBER:He was simply, you know –
CHORUS MEMBER: Penis –
CHORUS MEMBER: Had!

Teevan also introduces an original choral ode about the goddess Demeter losing her daughter Persephone that functions as analogue for Klytaimnestra losing Iphigenia, whose situation is also painted up by the quotation (in the introductory material) of Yeats's sonnet 'Leda and the Swan': since Leda seems to put on knowledge with Zeus's power,[17] we may infer that Iphigenia too was granted a type of knowledge – Greek victory? – when she was sacrificed.

3

A distinguished novelist and short story writer who has over many decades portrayed the experience of women in a powerful way,[18] Edna O'Brien has 'adapted' Euripides' play *Iphigenia in Aulis* under the title *Iphigenia*.[19] Her play premiered at the Crucible Theatre in Sheffield in February 2003 in a performance that lasted 75 minutes and so exemplified Greek brevity. Like many modern critics, O'Brien believes that Euripides 'now is recognized as the greatest of that triad of Athenian giants', and sees him as 'the dramatist, along with Shakespeare, who delved most deeply into the doings and passions of men and women'. O'Brien also views Euripides as a radical figure who questions received ideas, as 'the scourge of his native Athens'[20] (she is too uncritical of the notoriously unreliable biographies of Euripides).[21]

O'Brien realizes that in *Iphigenia in Aulis* there can be only one outcome, the sacrifice of Iphigenia by her father Agamemnon, but notes that 'each voice, each need, each nuance is beautifully and thoroughly rendered'.[22] In her *Iphigenia*, O'Brien makes a number of radical changes to Euripides. Her introduction of the Witch and the prophet Calchas as speaking characters serves to make very explicit the dramatic situation at the start of *Iphigenia in Aulis*: the Witch explains that the gods do not provide wind for the Greek fleet to go to Troy; Calchas states that the sacrifice of Iphigenia will bring victory over Troy to the Greeks. A further innovation is that O'Brien divides the Chorus of Women – young, excited, married – into six young Girls who have a sexual interest in Greek warriors such as Achilles that serves to point up the theme of Helen's adultery; as the Sixth Girl, who wishes for a relationship with Agamemnon, says, 'Women can learn marvellous things from captivating women'.[23] It is this Sixth Girl who first tells Clytemnestra that Iphigenia is to be killed (as in Euripides, the Old Man does so later).

O'Brien's Scene Two introduces a domestic scene between Clytemnestra, Iphigenia, her sister and a Nurse that renders more poignant the impending death of Iphigenia by heavily stressing the theme of her (supposed) marriage to Achilles, not least because she starts to menstruate for the first time. Equally dramatic moments follow when Agamemnon has finally accepted that Iphigenia must be killed – '*Agamemnon* hits his head against the wall, again and again' – and when Agamemnon grips Clytemnestra to convey his resolve about Iphigenia's supposed marriage: 'She starts to bite his hands to free her own; the bite is both erotic and determined.' At this point, O'Brien (unlike Euripides) attacks war : 'War. War. War. Why are men so enamoured of war?'[24]

At the end of *Iphigenia*, O'Brien brings on stage the goddess Artemis (speaking through the Witch) who has demanded the sacrifice of Iphigenia. The appearance of a deity at the end of a Greek tragedy – *the deus ex machina* – is designed to bring about a resolution of the play's central issue – as we have seen with Herakles in Sophocles' *Philoctetes*. But here the ending is ambivalent: on the one hand, Artemis accepts that Iphigenia is to die; on the other hand, she glances at the interpolated happy ending by saying to Iphigenia that 'When you have fulfilled your destiny/You shall be raised among the blessed'.[25]

O'Brien's play does not end with the killing of Iphigenia: the chorus of Young Girls prophesy that Clytemnestra and her lover Aegisthus will murder Agamemnon when he returns victorious from Troy with his concubine Cassandra. The death of a young girl will be paid for with the death of an older man – which seems a fitting ending for an author who has devoted so much space to the troubled intricacies of relationships between women and men.

---

[1] For *Iphigenia in Aulis* see C.A.E. Luschnig, *Tragic Aporia: A Study of Euripides' Iphigenia at Aulis* (Berwick: Aureal Publications, 1988).

[2] D.L. Page, *Actor's Interpolations in Greek Tragedy: Studied with Reference to Euripides' 'Iphigenia in Aulis'* (Oxford: Oxford University Press, 1934); J. Diggle, *Euripides Fabulai III* (Oxford: Oxford University Press, 1994).

[3] J. Morwood, *Euripides, Bacchae and Other Plays* (Oxford: Oxford University Press, 1999), p. 97.

4 Aristotle, *Poetics* 1454a. Translation by M. Heath.

5 For Iphigenia's change of mind see Luschnig (note 1), p. 53; pp. 105-08; p. 124; H. Siegel, *Hermes* 108(1980), pp. 300-21.

6 *ibid.*, p. 106.

7 *Three Tragedies by Renaissance Women*, ed. D. Purkiss (Harmondsworth: Penguin, 1998), contains Lady Jane Lumley's *The Tragedie of Iphigenia*.

8 For Cacoyannis' film *Iphigenia* see M. McDonald in *Classical Myth and Culture in the Cinema*, ed. M.M. Winkler (New York: Oxford University Press, 2001), pp. 90-101. For images of the film see *ibid.*, pp. 102-17.

9 Colin Teevan, *Iph ...* (London: Nick Hern Books, 1999).

10 Teevan (note 9), p. xiii.

11 *ibid.*, p. xiv; p. xviii; p. xiii.

12 *ibid.*, p. xiv; p. xv.

13 B. Arkins, *Rivista di studi Vittoriani* 2(1997), pp. 51-71.

14 Teevan (note 9), p. 41; pp. 18-19.

15 *ibid.*, p. xix-xx.

16 *ibid.*, pp. 22-23.

17 B. Arkins, *Builders of My Soul: Greek and Roman Themes in Yeats* (Gerrards Cross 1990), pp. 99-100.

18 For Edna O'Brien see, e.g., C.H. Mahony, *Contemporary Irish Literature* (London:Macmillan, 1998), pp. 210-15; for an interview with O'Brien by Helen Thompson see *Irish Women Writers Speak Out*, eds. C. Moloney and H. Thompson (Syracuse: Syracuse University Press, 2003), pp. 197-205.

19 Iphigenia by Euripides Adapted by Edna O'Brien (London 2003).

20 *ibid.*, p. vii; p. vi; p. vi.

21 M. Lefkowitz, *The Lives of the Greek Poets* (London: Duckworth, 1981).

22 O'Brien (note 9), p. vi.

23 *ibid.*, pp. 9-10.

24 *ibid.*, p. 22; p. 25; p. 25.

25 *ibid.*, p. 37.

12 | Aeschylus' *Oresteia*

1

Aeschylus' *Oresteia* trilogy[1] – *Agamemnon, Choephori, Eumenides* – can be understood only by examining the disastrous history of the most dysfunctional family in Greek tragedy, the house of Atreus. Since members of this family carry on a vendetta that endures over many generations, the central moral issue of the *Oresteia* is the nature of Justice (*Dike*): does Justice lie in an endless sequence of revenge killings? ('the doer suffers') Or can some other way out of the impasse be found? As the Chorus ask at the end of *Choephori*, Where will it end? – where will it sink to sleep and rest,/this murderous hate, this Fury?'[2]

The history of the house of Atreus involves the most spectacular list of crimes: murder, infanticide, cannibalism, seduction, incest, treachery, bribery. To begin with, Tantalus of Lydia fed the gods the flesh of his son Pelops (they 'tantalize' him in Hades with unavailable food and drink). The reconstituted Pelops wanted to marry Hippodameia and, to do so, had to outdistance her father Oinomaus in a chariot-race; receiving help from Myrtilus who crippled Oinomaus, Pelops won, but then refused to reward Myrtilus who cursed him. This curse is then manifested in the sons of Pelops, Atreus and Thyestes. Thyestes seduced Aerope, the wife of Atreus, who banished him; Atreus then recalled Thyestes, but served up to him the flesh of his own children. Thyestes fled, married his own daughter Pelopia, and became the father of Aegisthus. Since Agamemnon was the son of Atreus, enmity between him and Aegisthus is ensured.

Aeschylus' *Oresteia* begins in *Agamemnon* with the fall of Troy, the return of Agamemnon to Greece, and his bringing with him the Trojan prophet Cassandra as mistress; he had already aroused the anger of his wife Clytemnestra by sacrificing their daughter Iphigenia in order to get the Greeks to Troy. Clytemnestra and Aegisthus become lovers, and she kills Agamemnon – as well as Cassandra – on his return (after he is arrogant enough to walk on a purple carpet); she is possessed by 'our savage ancient spirit of revenge'.3 In the second play of the trilogy the *Choephori*, the conflict between genders continues: instructed to seek revenge by the god Apollo, Agamemnon's son Orestes returns to Argos after years of exile, and kills both Aegisthus and his mother Clytmnestra. But the Furies, ancient chthonic goddesses, daughters of the Night who avenge crimes within the family and especially matricide, arrive to haunt Orestes, who flies from them. Orestes is told in the third play *Eumenides* to seek justice in Athens from the goddess Athena, but is pursued there by the Furies. Athena refers judgement on the cases of Orestes and the Furies to a tribunal of Athenian judges (this is the Athenian court of the Areopagus that tried murder cases). After the tribunal hears the two cases, the votes are equal and the defendant Orestes is acquitted (as was Athenian practice in the fifth century). The Furies are then won over by Athena's promise to them of a new home in Athens, where they will turn into the Kindly Ones, *Eumenides*.

Aeschylus' *Oresteia* won the first prize at the Great Dionysia in 458 BC. Vital here is what Jones rightly calls 'Aeschylus' achievement in weaving round the body of the *oikos* (house) a seamless garment of sin-begotten and sin-begetting action in which the individual threads lose themselves within the whole'.4 That whole crucially involves a movement away from the culture of revenge, of an eye for an eye, to a culture of legal justice. Now Justice (*Dike*) is the law.5

2

Irish appropriation of Aeschylus' *Oresteia* takes the form of a translation of the three plays by Edward and Christine Longford, a translation of *Agamemnon* by Louis MacNeice, and loose adaptations set in the modern world by Marina Carr in *Ariel* and by Tom Murphy in *The Sanctuary Lamp*.

In a new translation by Edward Longford (*Agamemnon* and *Drink Offering*) and by his wife Christine (*The Furies*),6 the *Oresteia* was played on the same night at the Gate Theatre in Dublin in 1933 with a cast of fifty (Michael MacLiammoir played Orestes and Hilton Edwards Aegisthus). The Longfords, who both read Classics at Oxford, saw the theme of the *Oresteia* as 'the replacement of the blood-feud by human justice under divine sanction',[7] and aimed to provide in an easy accessible form 'what is, beyond doubt one of the greatest, as one of the earliest of dramatic works'.[8] But the Longfords' trilogy was a commercial disaster.

The Longfords assert that their translation of the *Oresteia* 'was frankly prepared for stage use' and that 'it reads easily'. Certainly, the translation has considerable merits: the register of language is clearly modern, and the use of iambic pentameter in the spoken parts of the plays works well. But the employment of rhyme in the choral parts tends towards the ludicrous: 'Priam's towers shall fall,/within his wall/Shall doom destroy his substance all'.[9] The obvious objection to rhyme is that it does not exist in Greek and Latin poetry, but the central problem with rhyme in the modern world is that it is outmoded and to be effective nowadays usually requires an ironic inflection (as with Tony Harrison and Derek Mahon).

<h1 style="text-align:center">3</h1>

Louis MacNeice's translation of Aeschylus' *Agamemnon*[10] was put on in London by the Group Theatre in 1936 (with music by Benjamin Britten) and published in the same year. MacNeice was very conscious that this play was to be *staged*: he asserted that 'I have written this translation primarily for the stage' and wanted it to read 'like a live play' (he also wished to assist the audience by having a drop-curtain 'with a family tree in the middle').[11] Unfortunately, one aspect of the staging was very problematic: the desire of the director Rupert Doone for originality ensured that the actors were dressed in a bizarre modern fashion, so that the Chorus wore dinner jackets, Agamemnon a jester's cap, and Aegisthus 'a Christmas cracker helmet and black evening cape'.[12] These excesses caused the elderly Yeats to remark to E. R. Dodds (newly appointed as Regius Professor of Greek at Oxford) that 'We are assisting, my dear Dodds, at the death of tragedy'.[13]

But Yeats also pointed out that MacNeice's translation deserved a better production. This translation of *Agamemnon* is in fact very fine and is stated by Hugh Lloyd-Jones (Dodd's successor at Oxford) to be 'the most successful version of any Greek tragedy that anyone in this country has yet produced'.[14] MacNeice's aim was to write in a register of language that is modern, strong and clear, and that therefore tones down the exuberance of Aeschylus: 'I have tried to make this translation vigorous, intelligible, and homogenous. I have avoided on the whole poetic or archaic diction and any diction or rhythm too reminiscent of familiar English models'.[15]

MacNeice succeeds very well in this endeavour, producing a translation that is 'genuinely poetic in a lean and sinewy way'. Take, for example, the speech of the Herald (lines 555-62) that suggests the conditions of World War I:[16]

> If I were to tell you of our labours, our hard lodging,
> The sleeper on crowded decks, the scanty blankets,
> Tossing and groaning, rations that never reached us -
> And the land too gave matter for mere disgust,
> For our beds lay under the enemy's walls,
> Continuous drizzle from the sky, dews from the marshes,
> Rotting our clothes, filling our hair with lice.

Such emphatic language ensures that MacNeice makes us aware of the central themes of *Agamemnon* such as the curse of the House of Atreus, the masculine daring of Clytemnestra, the approaching doom of Agamemnon. Indeed these themes of family may relate to MacNeice's own life: his mother died when he was very young; and his wife left him for another man.[17]

4

The fortunes of the house of Atreus as presented in Aeschylus' *Oresteia* lie behind Marina Carr's play *Ariel*[18] that premiered at the Abbey Theatre in Dublin in October 2002 and is set in the Irish Midlands (whose dialect is spoken in the play). The analogue for Agamemnon's killing of his daughter Iphigenia is found in the modern world when an Irish politician named Fermoy Fitzgerald kills his daughter Ariel on the day of her sixteenth birthday in order to advance his career. Hence his wife Frances says to him 'You laid my daughter on an altar of power', but it is never clear why this 'sacrifice to God' is necessary. Yet Fermoy's brother Boniface, a monk with whom he has many discussions about religion, has some sense of what is involved: 'Is ud some suurt a pagan calf calf ritual or are we talkin' something far older and more sinister here?' Indeed Fermoy's view of God is, for the Archbishop's office, 'ancient, barbaric, and will take us back to the caves'.[19]

Fermoy, who becomes a government minister, has other links to Greece: he owns a 'big house wud the Grake colums'; he sees himself in a dream 'dinin wud Alexander the Great, Napoleon and Caesar'; he champions Sparta's harsh treatment of handicapped babies: 'In Sparta they were left on the side a the hill and that ں where I'll leave em when I've the reins'.[20]

Just as a bloody history characterizes the dysfunctional house of Atreus, so the house of Fermoy Fitzgerald is pervaded by dark secrets. Fermoy's father killed his mother and (with Fermoy's help), placed her at the bottom of Cuura Lake (where Ariel also is), while her sister, Aunt Sarah, was having an affair with her brother-in-law. Fermoy's political rival Hanaffin spots the resemblance:[21] 'You were forged in a bloodbath, Fitzgerald, and the son elles carries the father somewhere inside of him', but Fermoy ensures that a scandal about Hanaffin becomes known, with the result that he commits suicide. The peculiarity of the family is further stressed by the fact that Frances Fitzgerald is still breastfeeding her ten year old son Stephen.

When Frances Fitzgerald comes to realize that Fermoy has killed their daughter Ariel, she repeatedly stabs her husband, as Clytemnestra murders Agamemnon; Frances further resembles Clytemnestra because she dreams she has been breastfeeding a snake in the shape of Stephen, the Orestes figure. But it is the Electra figure Elaine – of whom Frances says 'Seems to me we been battling a thousand year'[22] – who, at the end of the play, kills her mother because she is wishes to bury Ariel with Fermoy. Hence Carr's *Ariel* re-enacts the tit-for-tat killing of Aeschylus' plays *Agamemnon* and *Libation-Bearers*, but signally fails to reproduce the resolution of *Eumenides*. In the world of Carr, 'the Aeschylus of Offaly', tragedy remains tragic.

5

One of Ireland's leading contemporary dramatists, Tom Murphy has in his play *The Sanctuary Lamp* produced a modern adaptation of the *Oresteia* trilogy of Aeschylus.[23] Contrasting Murphy's play with other modern adaptations by Eugene O'Neill (*Mourning Becomes Electra*), by Sartre (*The Flies*), and by Eliot (*The Family Reunion*), Fintan O'Toole rightly maintains that *The Sanctuary Lamp* is 'the only modern version of the *Oresteia* which includes its political, psychological, and religious themes, and, more importantly, achieves the same reconciliation of the three which Aeschylus does'.[24]

Set in an unnamed modern city, *The Sanctuary Lamp* deals with characters who belong to 'the marginal sphere of the dispossessed',[25] and who exemplify Murphy's familiar theme of the disintegration of the family, a theme that is also of course Aeschylean. Hence Murphy's character Harry is Agamemnon, whose wife Olga (Clytemnestra) has been stolen by Francisco (an Irish Aegisthus) and whose daughter Teresa (Iphigenia) has died. But Harry is also Orestes, Murphy assigning characters several different Greek roles: he takes refuge in a Catholic Church like Orestes at the Temple of Apollo in Delphi; he calls, like Orestes, on the 'Lord of Death'; and he exacts his revenge by leaving the circus troupe and by physically attacking Francisco (Olga's suicide is a substitute for murder).

The religious aspect of the *Oresteia* as seen in the hymn to Zeus, and in the appearance of the deities Apollo, Athena, and the Furies is transformed in *The Sanctuary Lamp* into an analysis of a specific religious institution, the Roman Catholic Church, the action being set in a Catholic Church, presided over by a Monsignor, and with a sanctuary lamp, symbol of the presence of God, at its centre. The older bleak form of religion that presides over violent disruption in the family and that is represented in Aeschylus by the Furies becomes in *The Sanctuary Lamp* the life-denying form of Christianity espoused by Catholic priests. Aeschylus' new progressive religion embodied in Apollo becomes a kind of Blakean reversal of the values of institutional Catholicism. For the wider political context of a Greek royal family, Murphy substitutes a pretentious middle class in comparison with whom the circus characters are authentic.

The *Eumenides* comes into play when Francisco, now an Apollo-figure, seeks to establish a new religion which banishes 'life-denying' Catholic priests that he sees as Furies, agents of revenge. Indeed in the new order, Harry, who imagines that the dismembered family will come together again, forgives Francisco, and they plan to leave together. Aeschylus has enabled Murphy in *The Sanctuary Lamp* to move beyond his usual preoccupation with the difficulties of the family and of institutional religion to paint a brighter future, a reconciliation that is both Greek and Christian.

---

[1] For Aeschylus' *Oresteia* see, e.g., R. Fagles and W.B. Stanford, *Aeschylus – The Oresteia* (Harmondsworth: Penguin, 1977), pp. 13-97;
S. Goldhill, *Aeschylus – The Oresteia* (Cambridge: Cambridge University Press, 2004).

[2] Fagles (note 1), p. 226.

[3] *ibid.*, p. 165.

4 J. Jones, *On Aristotle and Greek Tragedy* (Stanford: Stanford University Press, 1980), p. 94.

5 For another view see Goldhill (note 1).

6 The Earl of Longford and Christine Longford, *The Oresteia of Aischulos*, (Dublin/Oxford: Hodge, Figgis and Co, 1933). For comment see J. Cowell, *No Profit but the Name – The Longfords and the Gate Theatre*, Dublin, 1988, pp. 93-94.

7 Longfords (note 6), p. 6.

8 Longfords, quoted in Cowell (note 6), p. 93.

9 *ibid.*, p. 16.

10 Louis MacNeice, *The Agamemnon of Aeschylus* (London: Faber & Faber, 1967). For comment see W.B. Stanford in T. Brown and A. Reid, *Time Was Away: The World of Louis MacNeice* (Dublin: Gill & Macmillan, 1974), pp. 63-66; M. Sidnell in *Greek Tragedy and its Legacy*, eds. M. Cropp, E. Fanthem, S.E. Scully (Calgary: Calgary University Press, 1986), pp. 323-35; E. Spiliopoulou, *Classical Influences in Louis MacNeice's Work* (Diss – Southampton 1989), pp. 173-241.

11 J. Stallworthy, *Louis MacNeice* (London: Faber & Faber, 1995), pp. 194-185.

12 Anonymous critic, quoted *ibid.*, p. 195.

13 E.R. Dodds, *Missing Persons* (Oxford: Oxford University Press, 1977), p. 132.

14 Lloyd-Jones, quoted *ibid.*, p. 116.

15 MacNeice, quoted in Stallworthy (note 11), p. 194.

16 MacNeice (note 10), pp. 31-32.

17 K. Younger, *Pages* 5(1998), pp. 187-97.

18 Marina Carr, *Ariel* (Oldcastle: Gallery Press, 2002). For comment see F. O'Toole in *The Theatre of Marina Carr*, eds. C. Leeney and A. McMullan (Dublin: Carysfort Press, 2003), pp. 89-91; C. Leeney in *The UCD Aesthetic*, ed. A. Roche (Dublin: UCD Press, 2005), pp. 265-73.

19 Carr (note 18), p. 58; p. 18; p. 19; p. 43.

20 *ibid.*, p. 32; p. 14; p. 18.

21 *ibid.*, p. 33.

22 *ibid.*, p. 66.

23 Tom Murphy, *The Sanctuary Lamp* (Dublin: Gallery Press, 1984). For comment on Murphy, see A. Roche, *Contemporary Irish Drama* (Dublin: Gill & Macmillan, 1994); F. O'Toole, *Tom Murphy – The Politics of Magic* (Dublin: New Island Books, 1994). For *The Sanctuary Lamp* see M. McDonald, *Ancient Sun, Modern Light: Greek Drama on the Modern Stage* (New York: Columbia University Press, 1992), pp. 171-85; O'Toole, *op. cit.*, pp. 184-207; A Poulain in *Talking About Tom Murphy*, ed. N. Grene (Dublin: Carysfort Press, 2002), pp.41-56; S. Richards, *ibid.*, pp. 57-65.

24 O'Toole (note 23), pp. 203-04.

25 Poulain (note 23), p. 41.

13 | Aeschylus' *Prometheus Bound*

1

The tragedy *Prometheus Bound*,[1] which is probably not by Aeschylus,[2] deals with the mythological figure of Prometheus ('Forethinker') who was a Titan, an older god of the generation before the Olympian gods. Although Prometheus fought on the side of the Olympian gods against the Titans, he became a champion of human beings against the Olympians, and taught them various skills such as carpentry, architecture, metallurgy, navigation, the domestication of animals, and the interpretation of omens (Prometheus was honoured in Athens with an altar, torchrace and festival). When Zeus deprived men of fire – necessary for cooking, heating, and rudimentary technology – Prometheus gave it back to them. Zeus then has Prometheus nailed to a lonely rock in the Caucasus, when he is to suffer great pain for as long as Zeus wishes. From this story, we see that Zeus is a harsh, implacable, irresponsible, violent tyrant; while Prometheus, who is knowledgeable and clever, is a symbol of those who champion the oppressed, and a figure dear to radical thinkers such as Shelley, who could not bear to see Prometheus subservient to Zeus and, in his play *Prometheus Unbound*, has him released.

In *Prometheus Bound*, Zeus is angry at Prometheus for his theft of fire, and orders Hephaistos, the god of fire, together with the figures of Kratos (Power) and Bia (Violence) to nail him down in Scythia. This setting of Scythia relates to Prometheus in two contrasting ways: on the one hand, the remote, untamed land of Scythia represents the opposite of Prometheus in his role of bringing technological progress on the other hand, the innocent, well-governed Scythians complement Prometheus' role as civilizing hero.³ Various figures, who help to keep the action going, arrive to comfort Prometheus: the Chorus of Oceanids, daughter of the Titan Oceanus, and Oceanus himself, a conformer who offers to intercede with Zeus, if Prometheus will moderate his approach; Prometheus refuses, being close to an obstinate Sophoclean hero. In a development original to the author, Io, who has been subjected to Zeus's lust and Hera's anger, arrives; she too has been the victim of tyranny.

Prometheus tells Io about her descendant Herakles who will eventually release him – much is made in the play of revelation – and about the fatal marriage that possibly awaits Zeus: whoever marries the sea-nymph Thetis, as Zeus wished to do, would produce a son greater than the father.

The god Hermes, the messenger of Zeus, enters and requires Prometheus to tell Zeus about the marriage to Thetis, but Prometheus refuses. As a result, Prometheus is plunged into Tartarus, a part of the underworld where the wicked suffer punishment for their misdeeds, and especially those who have committed some outrage against the gods. This ending to the tragedy *Prometheus Bound* sees Zeus enjoying complete victory over Prometheus, but a second play *Prometheus Freed* that came after it, deals with the final release of Prometheus from the Orphic Wheel of Necessity. It is possible that, in a further play, Zeus and Prometheus were reconciled.

2

Irish appropriation of *Prometheus Bound* takes the form of a 'version' by Tom Paulin called *Seize the* Fire.⁴ Important in Paulin are the title, the epigraph, and the prevailing brevity. Paulin's title *Seize the Fire* directs us not to Prometheus' imprisonment by Zeus, but to his providing human beings with the crucial gift of fire. Paulin's epigraph from Marx also stresses the importance of Prometheus as a champion of mankind, as a kind of humanist saint: 'Prometheus is the foremost saint and martyr in the philosopher's calendar.' At 33 pages of text, Paulin appears to match the brevity of *Prometheus Bound*'s 1093 lines, but his pervasive use of a very short line makes *Seize a Fire* seem a good deal shorter than the original. As seen in this extract from an early speech of Prometheus:⁵

> The secret source of fire and heat –
> that one, primal,

Idea of all ideas,
I searched it out –
so delicate and brittle
I hid it in a cusp of fennel,
a single spark
inside that aromatic
greeny-white bulb
I swim like a mullet
with a hook bedded
in its soft myth ...

Paulin preserves the invariant core of *Prometheus Bound* that stresses the tyranny of Zeus and the benevolence of Prometheus to human beings. Hence Prometheus asserts that 'Zeus hijacked both the history/and the state we made', and 'Had I not stole the fire/every last human body/would be stacked up dead here'.[6] But what makes *Seize the Fire* new is Paulin's relentless modernizing of ancient mythical materialism in both language and theme. In Athenian tragedy, obscenity was outlawed (it was permitted in comedy, as in Aristophanes), but Paulin uses contemporary obscenities freely 'shit'; 'tit'; 'to fuck you'.[7] Specially graphic is Io's account of Zeus's lust for her:[8]

and this buzz you hear
that's the song of his prick.
It's glued to my body
just like you're tied to that stake.
A hard high scream it is
that shaves and shapes me.
It flays my legs, lips, tits, bum,
then prick, prick, pricks me!

In terms of theme, Paulin employs contemporary images to express the authority of Zeus and the undermining of that authority. Hence Prometheus characterizes the Olympian gods in terms of the modern totalitarian state:

The gods of our new mythology are all generals and politicians. I helped them get power. I watched them drive in stretched limos to ceremonies where they made speeches and then awarded each other honours, titles, medals, stars, brownie points.

Hence Prometheus envisages a disastrous undermining of Zeus's power in terms of a contemporary political crisis: 'tanks on the lawn, news blackouts; 'food shortages'; 'martial music on the radio'.[9]

[1] M. Griffith, ed., *Aeschylus – Prometheus Bound* (Cambridge: Cambridge University Press, 1983); G. Thompson in *Oxford Readings in Greek Tragedy*, ed. E. Segal (Oxford: Oxford University Press, 1988), pp. 104-22.

[2] M. Griffith, *The Authenticity of Prometheus Bound* (Cambridge: Cambridge University Press, 1977).

[3] E. Hall, *Inventing the Barbarian* (Oxford: Oxford University Press, 1991), p. 114.

[4] Tom Paulin, *Seize the Fire* (London: Faber & Faber, 1990).

[5] Paulin (note 4), p. 9.

[6] *ibid.*, p. 21; p. 11.

[7] *ibid.*, p. 11; p. 33; p. 41.

[8] *ibid.*, p. 35.

[9] *ibid.*, p. 29; pp. 13-14.

Select Bibliography

Abbott, V., 'How It Was: Desmond Egan and Samuel Beckett' in *The Poet and His Work – Desmond Egan*, ed. H. Kenner (Northern Lights: Orono, 1990), pp. 44-53.

Adorno, T., *Negative Dialectics* (London: Routledge, 1973).

Albrecht, M. Von, 'Bernard Shaw and the Classics', *Classical & Modern Literature* 8 (1987), pp. 33-46 and 105-114.

Anouilh, Jean, *Antigone* (Paris: Bordas, 1984).

Arkins, B., 'Tradition Reshaped: Language and Style in Euripides' *Medea* 1-9, Ennius, *Medea Exul* 1-9 and Catullus 64. 1-30', *Ramus* II (1982), pp. 116-33.

---, 'Yeats's Version of Colonus' Praise', *Classical & Modern Literature* 7 (1986), pp. 39-42.

---, 'A Classical Perspective: Yeats's *King Oedipus* by Druid, *Theatre Ireland* 14 (1988), pp. 22-3.

---, 'The Final Lines of Sophocles' *King Oedipus*' – *Classical Quarterly* 38 (1988), pp. 555-58.

---, 'A Stage Direction in Yeats's *King Oedipus*', *Révue de Littérature Comparée*63 (1989), pp. 85-6.

---, *Builders of My Soul: Greek and Roman Themes in Yeats* (Gerrards Cross: Colin Smythe, 1990).

---, 'Greek Themes in Donna Tartt's *The Secret History, Classical & Modern Literature* 15 (1995), pp. 281-87.

---, 'Heavy Seneca': 'His Influence on Shakespeare's Tragedies', *Classics Ireland* 2 (1995), pp. 1-16.

---, 'Women in Irish Appropriation of Greek Tragedy' in *Amid Our Troubles – Irish Versions of Greek Tragedy*, eds. M. McDonald & J. M. Walton (London: Methuen, 2002), pp. 198-212.

---, 'Irish Appropriation of Sophocles' *Antigone* and Philoctetes' in *The Languages of Ireland*, eds. M. Cronin & C. O'Cuilleanáin (Dublin: Four Courts Press, 2003), pp. 167-78.

---, *Hellenising Ireland: Greek and Roman Themes in Modern Irish Literature* (Newbridge: Goldsmith Press, 2005).

Aylen, L., *Greek Tragedy and the Modern World* (London: Methuen, 1964).

Baldry, H.C., *The Greek Tragic Theatre* (London: Chatto-Windus, 1971).

Barlow, S., *Euripides – The Trojan Women* (Warminister: Aris & Phillips, 1986).

Barrett, W.S., *Euripides – Hippolytus* (Oxford: Oxford University Press, 1964).

Bassnett-Maguire, S., *Translation Studies* (London: Routledge, 1991).

Belli, A., *Ancient Greek Myths and Modern Drama* (London, 1968).

Bennett, S., *Theatre Audiences* (London: Routledge, 2003).

Borges, Jorge Louis, *The Aleph* (London, 1998).

Boyle, A.J., *Tragic Seneca: An Essay in the Theatrical Tradition* (London: Routledge, 1997).

Bremer, J. M., *Hamartia: Tragic Error in the Poetics of Aristotle and in Greek Tragedy* (Amsterdam: Rodopi, 1969).

Brower, R. A. (ed.), *On Translation* (New York: Oxford University Press, 1966).

Burnett, A. P., *Revenge in Attic and Later Tragedy* (Berkeley/Los Angeles: University of California Press, 1998).

Burke-Kennedy, Mary Elizabeth, *Oedipus* (Typescript 2000).

Cairns, D., 'Sophocles' *Antigone* by Brendan Kennelly', *Classics Ireland* 5 (1998), pp. 141-6.

Carr, Marina, *By the Bog of Cats...* (Oldcastle: Gallery Books, 1998).

---, *Ariel* (Oldcastle: Gallery Books, 2002).

---, *Plays One* (London: Faber & Faber, 1999).

Cave, R.A. (ed.) *Selected Plays of T.P. Murray* (Gerrards Cross/Washington D.C.: Colin Smythe, 1998).

---, 'After *Hippolytus*: Irish Versions of Phaedra's Story' in *Amid Our Troubles – Irish Versions of Greek Tragedy*, eds. M. McDonald & J. M. Walton (London: Methuen, 2002), pp. 101-27.

Clauss, J. J. & S. I. Johnston (eds.) *Medea. Essays on Medea in Myth, Literature, Philosophy, and Art* (Princeton: Princeton University Press, 1997).

Collard, C., *Euripides' Hecuba* (Warminister: Aris & Phillips, 1991).

Conacher, D. J., 'Some Profane Variations on a Tragic Theme', *Phoenix* 23 (1969), pp. 26-38.

Cowell, John, *No Profit But the Name: The Longfords and the Gate Theatre* (Dublin: O'Brien Press, 1988).

Croally, N.T., *Euripidean Polemic: the Trojan Women and the Function of Tragedy* (Cambridge: Cambridge University Press, 1994).

Cronin, M., *Translating Ireland: Translation, Languages, Culture* (Cork: Cork University Press, 1996).

Davies, J.K., *Democracy and Classical Greece* (London: Fontana, 1978).

Devereux, G., 'The Psychotherapy Scene in Euripides' *Bacchae*', *Journal of Hellenic Studies* 90 (1970), pp. 35-48.

---, 'The Self-Blinding of Oedipus', *Journal of Hellenic Studies* 93 (1973), pp. 36-49.

Diggle, J., *Euripides Fabulae III* (Oxford: Oxford University Press, 1994).

Dillon, J. & S.E. Wilmer, *Rebel Women – Staging Ancient Greek Drama Today* (London: Methuen, 2005).

Dodds, E.R., *The Greeks and the Irrational* (Berkeley: California University Press, 1951).

---, *Euripides – Bacchae* (Oxford: Oxford University Press, 1960).

---, *Missing Persons* (Oxford: Oxford University Press, 1977).

Dorn, K., *Players and Painted Stage – the Theatre of W.B. Yeats* (Brighton: The Harvester Press, 1984).

Dukakis, J. & N.C. Liebler (eds.) *Tragedy* (London: Longman, 1998).

Duncan, D., *Postcolonial Theory in Irish Drama from 1800 to 2000* (Lewiston: Edwin Mellon Press, 2004).

Eagleton, T., 'Unionism and Utopia: Seamus Heaney's *The Cure at Troy*' in *Theatre Stuff: Critical Essays on Contemporary Irish Theatre*, ed. E. Jordan (Dublin: Carysfort Press, 2000), pp.172-75.

---, *Sweet Violence – The Idea of the Tragic* (Oxford: Blackwell, 2003).

Easterling, P.E., 'The Infanticide in Euripides *Medea*', *Yale Classical Studies* 25 (1977), pp. 177-91.

---, (ed.) *The Cambridge Companion to Greek Tragedy* (Cambridge: Cambridge University Press, 1997).

Edmonds, L., *Oedipus* (Baltimore: The Johns Hopkins Press, 1996).

Egan, Desmond, *Euripides – Medea* (Newbridge: Goldsmith Press, 1991).

---, *Sophocles – Philoctetes* (Newbridge: Goldsmith Press, 1998).

---, *The Death of Metaphor* (Gerrards Cross: Colin Smythe, 1990).

Eliot, T.S., *Selected Essays* (New York, 1964).

Ellmann, R., *James Joyce* (Oxford: Oxford University Press, 1982).

Else, G.F., *Aristotle's Poetics* (Harvard: Harvard University Press, 1957).

Fagles, R., *Aeschylus – The Oresteia* (Harmondsworth: Penguin, 1984).

---, *Sophocles – The Three Theban Plays* (Harmondsworth: Penguin, 1984).

Fatoula, M.A. (OP), 'Suffering' in *The New Dictionary of Theology*, eds. J. A. Komanchak, M. Collins & D.A. Lane (Dublin: Gill and Macmillan, 1987).

Ferguson, F., *The Idea of a Theatre* (Princeton: Princeton University Press, 1949).

Finley, M.I. 'The Athenian Empire' in his *Economy and Society in Ancient Greece* (Harmondsworth: Penguin, 1983), pp. 41-61.

---, (ed.) *The Legacy of Greece* (Oxford: Oxford University Press, 1981).

Fitzgerald, G., 'Europe's Malleable Topos: Mythologizing Ancient Greece', *Ramus* 25 (1996), pp. 1-16.

Foley, H., *Ritual Irony: Poetry and Sacrifice in Euripides* (Ithaca/London: Cornell University Press, 1985).

---, *Female Acts in Greek Tragedy* (Princeton/Oxford: Princeton University Press, 2001).

Franklin, D. & J. Harrison, *Sophocles – Antigone* (Cambridge: Cambridge University Press), 2003.

Friel, Brian, *Selected Plays* (London: Faber & Faber, 1984).

Gardner, W.H. & N. MacKenzie,. (eds), *The Poems of Gerard Manley Hopkins* (Oxford: Oxford University Press, 1970).

Gibbs, A.M., *The Art and Mind of Shaw* (London, 1983).

Gilbert, H. & J. Tompkins, *Post-Colonial Drama* (London: Routledge, 1996).

Gilmartin, K., 'Talthybius in *The Trojan Women*', *American Journal of Philology* 91 (1970), pp. 213-22.

Golden, L. & Hardison, O. B. (Jr.), *Aristotle's Poetics* (Englewood Cliffs, N.J: Prentice-Hall, 1968).

Goldhill, S., *Reading Greek Tragedy* (Cambridge: Cambridge University Press, 1986).

---, *Who Needs Greek?* (Cambridge: Cambridge University Press, 2002).

---, *Aeschylus - The Oresteia* (Cambridge: Cambridge University Press, 2004).

Grob, F.D., 'Yeats's King Oedipus', *Journal of English and Germanic Philology* 71 (1972), pp. 336-54.

Grene, N., Bernard Shaw – A Critical View (London, 1984).

---, *The Politics of Irish Drama* (Cambridge: Cambridge University Press, 1999).

---, (ed.) *Talking About Tom Murphy* (Dublin: Carysfort Press, 2002).

Grennan, E. & R. Kitzinger, *Sophocles – Oedipus at Colonus* (New York: Oxford University Press, 2005).

Griffith, M., *Sophocles – Antigone* (Cambridge: Cambridge University Press, 2003).

---, *The Authenticity of the Prometheus Bound* (Cambridge: Cambridge University Press, 1977).

---, *Aeschylus – Prometheus Bound* (Cambridge: Cambridge University Press, 1983).

Hall, E., *Inventing the Barbarian* (Oxford: Oxford University Press, 1991).

---, with F. Macintosh & A. Wrigley, (eds) *Dionysus Since 69 – Greek Tragedy at the Dawn of the Third Millenium* (Oxford: Oxford University Press, 2005).

Halloran, M.R., *Hippolytus* (Warminister: Aris & Phillips, 1995).

Halliwell, S., *The Poetics of Aristotle* (London: Duckworth, 1987).

Hardy, B., 'The Wildness of Crazy Jane' in *Yeats, Sligo and Ireland*, ed. A. N. Jeffares (Gerrards Cross: Colin Smythe, 1980), pp. 31-55.

Harrison, Tony, *Dramatic Verse 1973-1985* (Newcastle-upon-Tyne: Bloodaxe, 1985).

Heaney, Seamus, *The Curse of Troy* (London: Faber & Faber, 1990).

---, *The Burial at Thebes* (London: Faber & Faber. 2004).

Heath, M., *Aristotle – Poetics* (London: Penguin, 1996).

Heidegger, M., 'The Ode on Man in Sophocles' *Antigone*' in *Sophocles*, ed. T. Woodward (Englewood Cliffs, N. J.: Prentice-Hall, 1966), pp. 86-100.

Henn, T. R., *The Harvest of Tragedy* (London: Methuen, 1966).

Henrichs, A., 'Why Should I Dance?' *Arion* 3 (1995), pp. 56-111.

Henry, D. & B. Walker, *The Mask of Power: Seneca's Tragedies and Imperial Rome* (Warminister: Aris & Phillips, 1985).

Herington, C.J., 'Senecan Tragedy', *Arion* 5 (1966), pp. 422-71.

Herodotus, *The Histories*.

Hester, D. A., 'Sophocles and the Unphilosophical', *Mnemosyne* 24 (1971), pp. 11-59.

Highet, G., *The Classical Tradition* (London: Oxford University Press, 1987).

Hornblower, S., *The Greek World 479-323 BC* (London: Duckworth 2002).

Johnston, D., *John Millington Synge* (New York/London 1965).

Jones, J., *On Aristotle and Greek Tragedy* (Stanford: University of California Press, 1980).

Joseph, S., *Medea in Late Twentieth-Century Theatre* (Diss: Washington, D.C., 2002).

Joyce, James, *Stephen Hero* (London: Granada, 1981).

---, *Occasional, Critical, and Political Writing*, ed. K. Barry (Oxford: Oxford University Press, 2000).

Kavanagh, Patrick, *Collected Poems* (London: Martin Brian & O'Keefe, 1973).

Kells, J. H., *Sophocles – Electra* (Cambridge: Cambridge University Press, 2000).

Kennelly, Brendan, *Medea* (Newcastle-upon-Tyne: Bloodaxe, 1991).

---, *The Trojan Women* (Newcastle-upon-Tyne: Bloodaxe, 1993).

---, *Antigone* (Newcastle-upon-Tyne: Bloodaxe, 1996).

---, *When Then is Now – Three Greek Tragedies* (Tarset: Bloodaxe, 2006).

Kiberd, D., *Inventing Ireland* (London: Jonathan Cape, 1995).

Kilroy, T. 'Theatrical Text and Literary Text' in *The Achievement of Brian Friel*, ed. A. Peacock (Gerrards Cross: Colin Smythe, 1993), pp. 93-7.

Kitto, H.D.F., *Form and Meaning in Drama* (London: Methuen, 1956).

Knox, B. M. W., *The Heroic Temper – Studies in Sophoclean Tragedy* (Berkeley/Los Angeles: University of California Press, 1966).

---, *Oedipus at Thebes* (New Haven/London: Yale University Press, 1998).

Lee, K.H., *Euripides – Troades* (London, 1976).

Leech, C., *Tragedy* (London: Methuen, 1969).

Leeney, C. & A. McMullan, (eds.), *The Theatre of Marina Carr* (Dublin: Carysfort Press, 2003).

Leeney, C., 'Marina Carr in *The UCD Aesthetic*, ed. A. Roche (Dublin: 2005), pp. 265-73.

Lefevere, A. (ed.), *Translation/History/Culture* (London: Routledge, 1992).

Lefkowitz, M., *The Lives of the Greek Poets* (London: Duckworth, 1981).

Liebregts, P. Th.R.G., *Centaurs in the Twilight – W. B. Yeats's Use of the Classical Tradition* (Amsterdam/Atlanta: Rodopi, 1993).

Lloyd, M., 'Euripides' The Trojan Women' *Classics Ireland* 1 (1994), pp. 54-60.

---, *The Agon in Euripides* (Oxford: Oxford University Press, 1992).

Lloyd-Jones, H., *Blood for the Ghosts* (London: Duckworth, 1982).

---, *Sophocles – Antigone, The Women of Trachis, Philoctetes, Oedipus at Colonus* (Cambridge, Mass./London: Harvard University Press, 2002).

Longford, Earl of & Christine Longford, *The Oresteia of Aischulos* (Dublin/Oxford, 1933).

Loraux, L., *Tragic Ways of Killing a Woman* (Cambridge, Mass.: Harvard University Press 1987).

Luschnig, C., *Time Holds the Mirror: A Study of Knowledge in Euripides' Hippolytus* (Leiden: Brill 1988).

---, *Tragic Aporia: A Study in Euripides' Iphigeneia in Aulis* (Berwick: Aureal Publications, 1988).

McDonagh, J., *Brendan Kennelly – A Host of Ghosts* (Dublin: The Liffey Press, 2004).

McDonald, M. & J.M. Walton, (eds.), *Amid Our Troubles – Irish Versions of Greek Tragedy* (London: Methuen, 2002).

McDonald, M., 'The Irish and Greek Tragedy', *ibid.*, pp. 37-86.

---, *Ancient Sun, Modern Light: Greek Drama on the Modern Stage* (New York: Columbia University Press, 1992).

---, '"A Bomb at the Door": Kennelly's *Medea*', *Éire – Ireland* XXVIII (2) (1993), pp. 129-37.

---, 'Seamus Heaney's "Cure at Troy: Politics and Poetry"', *Classics Ireland* 3 (1996), pp. 129-40.

---, 'Medea as Politician and Diva: Riding the Dragon into the Future' in *Medea: Essays on Medea in Myth, Literature, Philosophy and Art*, eds. J.J. Clauss & S.I. Johnston (Princeton: Princeton University Press, 1997).

---, 'Recent Irish Translations of Greek Tragedy: Derek Mahon's *Bacchai*; in *The Translation of Ancient Greek Drama into All the Languages of the World*, ed. E. Patrikiou (Athens: Desmoi lenter, 1998), pp 191-200.

---, 'Violent Words: Brian Friel's *Living Quarters:* after *Hippolytus*', *Arion* (Spring/Summer 1998), pp. 35-47.

---, 'Eye of the Camera, Eye of the Victim: *Iphigenia* by Euripides and Cacoyannis' in *Classical Myth and Culture in the Cinema*, ed. M.M. Winkler (Oxford: Oxford University Press, 2001), pp. 90-101.

MacKillop, I., *F. R. Leavis: A Life in Criticism* (London: Penguin, 1997).

Macleod, J., *Beginning Postcolonialism* (Manchester: Manchester University Press, 2000).

McCracken, K., 'Rage for a New Order: Brendan Kennelly's Play for Women' in *Dark Fathers into Light: Brendan Kennelly*, ed. R. Pine (Newcastle-upon-Tyne: Bloodaxe, 1994), pp. 114-47.

McMullan, A., 'Gender, Authority and Performance in Selected Plays by Contemporary Irish Women Playwrights' in *Theatre Stuff: Critical Essays on Contemporary Irish Theatre*, ed. E. Jordan (Dublin: Carysfort Press, 2000).

Macintosh, F., *Dying Acts – Death in Ancient Greek and Modern Irish Drama* (Cork: Cork University Press, 1994).

MacNeice, Louis, *The Collected Poems of Louis MacNeice*, ed. E.R. Dodds (London: Faber & Faber, 1968).

---, *The Poetry of W.B. Yeats* (London: Faber & Faber, 1967).

---, *The Agamemnon of Aeschylus* (London: Faber & Faber, 1967).

McGuinness, Frank, *Sophocles – Electra* (London: Faber & Faber, 1997).

---, *Euripides' Hecuba* (London: Faber & Faber, 2004).

Mahon, Derek, *The Bacchae* (Oldcastle: Gallery Press, 1991).

Mason, H., 'The Women of Trachis and Creative Translation' in *Ezra Pound*, ed. J. P. Sullivan (Harmondsworth: Penguin, 1970), pp. 279-310.

Mastronarde, D.J., *Euripides – Medea* (Cambridge: Cambridge University Press, 2002).

Mathews, Aidan, *Antigone* (1984).

---, *Trojans* (1995).

Meiggs, R., *The Athenian Empire* (Oxford: Oxford University Press, 1972).

Meir, C., 'Classical and Political Analogues in Heaney's *The Cure at Troy*' in *The Classical World and the Mediterranean*, eds. G. Serpillo & D. Badin (Cagliari: Tema, 1996).

Morash, C., *A History of Irish Theatre 1601-2000* (Cambridge: Cambridge University Press, 2002).

Morgan, M. M., *The Shavian Playground* (London, 1974).

Morwood, J., *Euripides – The Trojan Women and other Plays* (Oxford: Oxford University Press, 2000).

---, *Euripides – Bacchae and other Plays* (Oxford: Oxford University Press, 2002).

Mossman, J., *Wild Justice – A Study of Euripides' Hecuba* (Oxford: Clarendon Press 1995).

Munday, J., *Introducing Translation Studies* (London: Routledge, 2001).

Murphy, Thomas, *The Sanctuary Lamp* (Dublin: Gallery Press, 1984).

Murray, C., *Twentieth-Century Irish Drama* (Manchester: Manchester University Press, 1997).

---, 'Three Irish Antigones' in *Perspectives of Irish Drama and Theatre*, eds. J. Genet & R. Cave (Gerrards Cross: Colin Smythe, 1991, pp. 115-29.

Ní Annluain, C. (ed.), Reading the Future: Irish Writers in Conversation with Mike Murphy (Dublin: RTÉ, 2000).

Nietzsche, F., *The Birth of Tragedy* (1872).

Nussbaum, M., *The Fragility of Goodness* (Cambridge: Cambridge University Press, 1986).

Nuttall, A.D., *Why Does Tragedy Give Pleasure?* (Oxford: Clarendon Press, 2001).

O'Brien, Edna, *Iphigeneia by Euripides* (London: Metheun, 2003).

O'Hanlon, R., 'Brian Friel's Dialogue with Euripides' in *Theatre Stuff: Critical Essays on Contemporary Irish Theatre*, ed. E. Jordan (Dublin: Carysfort Press, 2000), pp. 107-21.

Orr, J. *Tragic Drama and Modern Society* (London, 1981).

O'Toole, F., *Tom Murphy – The Politics of Magic* (Dublin: New Island, 1994).

---, *Shakespeare is Hard, but so is Life* (London/New York: Granta Books, 2002).

---, Review of Marina Carr, *Ariel* in *The Theatre of Marina Carr*, eds. C. Leeney & A. MacMullan (Dublin: Carysfort Press, 2003).

Page, D.L., *Actor's Interpolations in Greek Tragedy with Reference to Euripides' Iphigeneia in Aulis* (Oxford: Oxford University Press, 1934).

---, *Euripides' Medea* (Oxford: Oxford University Press, 1978).

---, (ed.) *Letters of John Keats* (London, 1954).

Paulin, Tom, *Ireland and the English Crisis* (Newcastle-upon-Tyne: Bloodaxe 1984).

---, *The Riot Act* (London: Faber & Faber, 1985).

---, *Seize the Fire* (London: Faber & Faber, 1990).

Peacock, A., 'Translating the Past: Friel, Greece and Rome' in *The Achievement of Brian Friel*, ed. A. Peacock (Gerrards Cross: Colin Smythe, 1993), pp. 113-20.

Pelan, R., 'In a Class of their Own: Women in Theatre in Contemporary Ireland' in *(Post) Colonial Stages* ed. H. Gilbert (Hebden Bridge: Dangaroo Press, 1999), pp. 243-52.

Pichard-Cambridge, A. W., *The Dramatic Festivals of Athens* (Oxford: Oxford University Press, 1988).

Pilkington, L., *Theatre and the State in Twentieth-Century Ireland* (London: Routledge, 2001).

Pilling, J. (ed.) *The Cambridge Companion to Beckett* (Cambridge: Cambridge University Press, 1996).

Pine, R. (ed.), *Dark Fathers into Light – Brendan Kennelly* (Newcastle-upon-Tyne: Bloodaxe, 1994).

Pomeroy, S. B., *Goddesses, Whores, Wives, and Slaves* (London: Pimlico, 1994).

Poole, A., 'Total Disaster: Euripides; The Trojan Women' *Arion* 3 (1976), pp. 257-87.

---, *Tragedy* (Oxford: Oxford University Press, 2005).

Richards, I. A., *Principles of Literary Criticism* (London: Routledge, 1967).

Roche, A., 'Three Irish Antigones' in *Cultural Contexts and Literary Idiom in Contemporary Irish Literature*, ed. M. Kenneally (Gerrards Cross: Colin Smythe, 1988), pp. 221-50.

---, *Contemporary Irish Drama* (Dublin: Gill & Macmillan, 1994).

Sale, W., *Existentialism and Euripides* (Berwick: Aureal Publications, 1977).

Schlesinger, E., 'On Euripides' Medea' in *Euripides* ed. E. Segal (Englewood Cliffs, N. J.: Prentice-Hall, 1968), pp. 70-89.

Schull, R., 'The Preparation of King Oedipus, *The Arts in Ireland* 2 (1973), pp. 15-21.

Seaford R., *Euripides' Bacchae* (Warminister: Aris & Phillips, 1996).

Segal, C., 'Sophocles Praise of Man and the Conflicts of the *Antigone*' in *Sophocles*, ed. T. Woodard (Englewood Cliffs, N. J.: Prentice-Hall, 1966), pp. 62-85.

---, 'Shame and Purity in Euripides' *Hippolytus*', *Hermes* 98 (1970), pp. 278-99.

---, 'The Tragedy of the *Hippolytus*: The Waters of ocean and the Untouched Meadow', *Harvard Studies in Classical Philology* 70 (1965), pp. 117-69.

Shaw, George Bernard, *Major Barbara* (London: Penguin, n. d.).

Shaw, M., 'The Female Intruder', *Classical Philology* 70 (1975), pp. 255-66.

Siegel, H., 'Self-Delusion and the Volte-face of Iphigeneia in Euripides' "Iphigeneia at Aulis"', *Hermes* 108 (1980), pp. 300-21.

Silk, M. S. & Stern, J. P., *Nietzsche on Tragedy* (Cambridge: Cambridge University Press, 1981).

---, (ed.) *Tragedy and the Tragic* (Oxford: Oxford University Press, 1996).

Simon, S., *Gender in Translation* (London: Routledge, 1996).

Smith, Sydney, *Sherca* (Newark: Proscenium Press, 1979).

Sotto, W., *The Rounded Rite* (Lund: CWK Gleerup, 1985).

Sommerstein, A. H., *Greek Drama and Dramatists* (London: Routledge, 2002).

Soyinka, Wole, *Collected Plays I* (Oxford: Oxford University Press, 1973).

Spiliopoulou, E., *Classical Influences in Louis MacNeice's Work* (Diss.: Southampton, 1989).

Stallworthy, J., *Louis MacNeice* (London: Faber & Faber, 1995).

Steiner, G., *The Death of Tragedy* (New Haven: Yale University Press, 1996).

---, *Antigones* (Oxford: Oxford University Press, 1984).

---, *After Babel* (Oxford: Oxford University Press, 1998).

Stevens, Wallace, *Opus Posthumous*, ed. S.F. Morse (London, 1959).

Sullivan, J.P. (ed.) *Ezra Pound* (Harmondsworth: Penguin, 1970).

Synge, J.M., *Plays* (Oxford: Oxford University Press, 1969).

Tanner, G., 'The Dramas of T.S. Eliot and their Greek Models', *Greece & Rome* 17 (1970), pp. 123-34.

Tanner, M., *Nietzsche* (London: Fontana 1996).

Tartt, Donna, *The Secret History* (London: Penguin, 1992).

Teevan, Colin, *Euripides – Bacchai* (London: Oberon Books, 2002).

---, *Iph... – after Euripides 'Iphigeneia in Aulis'* (London: Nick Hern Books, 1999).

Thompson, G., 'Aeschylus' Prometheus Bound' in *Oxford Readings in Greek Tragedy*, ed. E. Segal (Oxford: Oxford University Press, 1988), pp. 104-22.

Thucydides, *History of the Peloponnesian War*.

Tilley, T.W., 'Evil, Problem of' in *The New Dictionary of Theology*, eds. J.A. Komonchak, M. Collins, & D.A. Lane (Dublin: Gill & Macmillan, 1987), pp. 360-63.

Tymoczko, M., *Translation in a Post-Colonial Context: Early Irish Literature in English Translation* (Manchester: Manchester University Press, 1999).

Vernant, J.-P., *Myth and Tragedy in Ancient Greece* (New York: Zone Books, 1990).

Vieira, E.R.P., 'Liberating Calibans' in *Postcolonial Translation*, eds. S. Bassnett & H. Trivedi (London: Routledge, 1999), pp. 95-113.

Walton, J.M., 'Hit or Myth: the Greeks and Irish Drama' in *Amid Our Troubles – Irish Versions of Greek Tragedy*, eds. M. McDonald & J. M. Walton (London: Methuen, 2002), pp. 3-36.

---, *Found in Translation – Greek Drama in English* (Cambridge: Cambridge University Press, 2007).

Watling, E. F., *Sophocles – Electra and other Plays* (Harmondsworth: Penguin, 1953).

West, M., *Ancient Greek Music* (Oxford: Oxford University Press, 1992).

Winkler, J.J. & F. Zeitlin, *Nothing to do with Dionysus: Athenian Drama in its Social Context* (Princeton: Princeton University Press, 1990).

Winnington-Ingram, R. P., *Euripides and Dionysus – An Interpretation of the Bacchae* (London: Bristol Classical Press, 2003).

Woolf, Virginia, *A Room of One's Own* (London: Flamingo, 1994).

---, *The Common Reader* (London: The Hogart Press, 1925).

Yeats, W.B., *A Vision* (London: T. Werner Laurie, 1925).

---, *Collected Plays* (London: Macmillan, 1960).

---, *Explorations* (London: Macmillan, 1962).

---, *Letters*, ed. A. Wade (London: Rupert Hart-Davis, 1950).

---, *Letters to Dorothy Wellesley* (London: Oxford University Press, 1964).

Index

Carysfort Press was formed in the summer of 1998. It receives annual funding from the Arts Council.

The directors believe that drama is playing an ever-increasing role in today's society and that enjoyment of the theatre, both professional and amateur, currently plays a central part in Irish culture.

The Press aims to produce high quality publications which, though written and/or edited by academics, will be made accessible to a general readership. The organisation would also like to provide a forum for critical thinking in the Arts in Ireland, again keeping the needs and interests of the general public in view.

The company publishes contemporary Irish writing for and about the theatre.

Editorial and publishing inquiries to:
Carysfort Press Ltd.,
58 Woodfield,
Scholarstown Road,
Rathfarnham,
Dublin 16,
Republic of Ireland.

T (353 1) 493 7383
F (353 1) 406 9815
E: info@carysfortpress.com
www.carysfortpress.com

HOW TO ORDER

TRADE ORDERS DIRECTLY TO:
CMD/BookSource
55A Spruce Avenue,
Stillorgan Industrial Park
Blackrock,
Co. Dublin

T: (353 1) 294 2560
F: (353 1) 294 2564
E: cmd@columba.ie

INDIVIDUAL ORDERS DIRECTLY TO:
eprint Ltd.
35 Coolmine Industrial Estate,
Blanchardstown, Dublin 15.
T: (353 1) 827 8860
F: (353 1) 827 8804 Order online @
E: books@eprint.ie
www.eprint.ie

FOR SALES IN NORTH AMERICA AND CANADA:
Dufour Editions Inc.,
124 Byers Road,
PO Box 7,
Chester Springs,
PA 19425,
USA

T: 1-610-458-5005
F: 1-610-458-7103

Alive in Time: The Enduring Drama of Tom Murphy

Ed. Christopher Murray

Almost 50 years after he first hit the headlines as Ireland's most challenging playwright, the 'angry young man' of those times Tom Murphy still commands his place at the pinnacle of Irish theatre. Here 17 new essays by prominent critics and academics, with an introduction by Christopher Murray, survey Murphy's dramatic oeuvre in a concerted attempt to define his greatness and enduring appeal, making this book a significant study of a unique genius.

ISBN 978-1-904505-45-7   €25

Performing Violence in Contemporary Ireland

Lisa Fitzpatrick

This interdisciplinary collection of fifteen new essays by scholars of theatre, Irish studies, music, design and politics explores aspects of the performance of violence in contemporary Ireland. With chapters on the work of playwrights Martin McDonagh, Martin Lynch, Conor McPherson and Gary Mitchell, on Republican commemorations and the 90th anniversary ceremonies for the Battle of the Somme and the Easter Rising, this book aims to contribute to the ongoing international debate on the performance of violence in contemporary societies.

ISBN 978-1-904505-44-0 (2009) €20

Ireland's Economic Crisis - Time to Act. Essays from over 40 leading Irish thinkers at the MacGill Summer School 2009

Eds. Joe Mulholland and Finbarr Bradley

Ireland's economic crisis requires a radical transformation in policymaking. In this volume, political, industrial, academic, trade union and business leaders and commentators tell the story of the Irish economy and its rise and fall. Contributions at Glenties range from policy, vision and context to practical suggestions on how the country can emerge from its crisis.

ISBN 978-1-904505-43-3 (2009) €20

Deviant Acts: Essays on Queer Performance

Ed. David Cregan

This book contains an exciting collection of essays focusing on a variety of alternative performances happening in contemporary Ireland. While it highlights the particular representations of gay and lesbian identity it also brings to light how diversity has always been a part of Irish culture and is, in fact, shaping what it means to be Irish today.

ISBN 978-1-904505-42-6 (2009) €20

Seán Keating in Context: Responses to Culture and Politics in Post-Civil War Ireland

Compiled, edited and introduced by Éimear O'Connor

Irish artist Seán Keating has been judged by his critics as the personification of old-fashioned traditionalist values. This book presents a different view. The story reveals Keating's early determination to attain government support for the visual arts. It also illustrates his socialist leanings, his disappointment with capitalism, and his attitude to cultural snobbery, to art critics, and to the Academy. Given the national and global circumstances nowadays, Keating's critical and wry observations are prophetic – and highly amusing.

ISBN 978-1-904505-41-9 €25

Dialogue of the Ancients of Ireland: A new translation of Acallam na Senorach

Translated with introduction and notes by Maurice Harmon

One of Ireland's greatest collections of stories and poems, The Dialogue of the Ancients of Ireland is a new translation by Maurice Harmon of the 12th century *Acallam na Senorach*. Retold in a refreshing modern idiom, the *Dialogue* is an extraordinary account of journeys to the four provinces by St. Patrick and the pagan Cailte, one of the surviving Fian. Within the frame story are over 200 other stories reflecting many genres – wonder tales, sea journeys, romances, stories of revenge, tales of monsters and magic. The poems are equally varied – lyrics, nature poems, eulogies, prophecies, laments, genealogical poems. After the *Tain Bo Cuailnge*, the *Acallam* is the largest surviving prose work in Old and Middle Irish.

ISBN: 978-1-904505-39-6 (2009) €20

Literary and Cultural Relations between Ireland and Hungary and Central and Eastern Europe

Ed. Maria Kurdi

This lively, informative and incisive collection of essays sheds fascinating new light on the literary interrelations between Ireland, Hungary, Poland, Romania and the Czech Republic. It charts a hitherto under-explored history of the reception of modern Irish culture in Central and Eastern Europe and also investigates how key authors have been translated, performed and adapted. The revealing explorations undertaken in this volume of a wide array of Irish dramatic and literary texts, ranging from *Gulliver's Travels* to *Translations* and *The Pillowman*, tease out the subtly altered nuances that they acquire in a Central European context.

ISBN: 978-1-904505-40-2 (2009) €20

Plays and Controversies: Abbey Theatre Diaries 2000-2005

By Ben Barnes

In diaries covering the period of his artistic directorship of the Abbey, Ben Barnes offers a frank, honest, and probing account of a much commented upon and controversial period in the history of the national theatre. These diaries also provide fascinating personal insights into the day-to- day pressures, joys, and frustrations of running one of Ireland's most iconic institutions.

ISBN: 978-1-904505-38-9 (2008)   €35

Interactions: Dublin Theatre Festival 1957-2007. Irish Theatrical Diaspora Series: 3

Eds. Nicholas Grene and Patrick Lonergan with Lilian Chambers

For over 50 years the Dublin Theatre Festival has been one of Ireland's most important cultural events, bringing countless new Irish plays to the world stage, while introducing Irish audiences to the most important international theatre companies and artists. Interactions explores and celebrates the achievements of the renowned Festival since 1957 and includes specially commissioned memoirs from past organizers, offering a unique perspective on the controversies and successes that have marked the event's history. An especially valuable feature of the volume, also, is a complete listing of the shows that have appeared at the Festival from 1957 to 2008.

ISBN: 978-1-904505-36-5   €25

The Informer: A play by Tom Murphy based on the novel by Liam O'Flaherty

The Informer, Tom Murphy's stage adaptation of Liam O'Flaherty's novel, was produced in the 1981 Dublin Theatre Festival, directed by the playwright himself, with Liam Neeson in the leading role. The central subject of the play is the quest of a character at the point of emotional and moral breakdown for some source of meaning or identity. In the case of Gypo Nolan, the informer of the title, this involves a nightmarish progress through a Dublin underworld in which he changes from a Judas figure to a scapegoat surrogate for Jesus, taking upon himself the sins of the world. A cinematic style, with flash-back and intercut scenes, is used rather than a conventional theatrical structure to catch the fevered and phantasmagoric progression of Gypo's mind. The language, characteristically for Murphy, mixes graphically colloquial Dublin slang with the haunted intricacies of the central character groping for the meaning of his own actions. The dynamic rhythm of the action builds towards an inevitable but theatrically satisfying tragic catastrophe. ' [The Informer] is, in many ways closer to being an original Murphy play than it is to O'Flaherty...' Fintan O'Toole.

ISBN: 978-1-904505-37-2 (2008)   €10

Shifting Scenes: Irish theatre-going 1955-1985

Eds. Nicholas Grene and Chris Morash

Transcript of conversations with John Devitt, academic and reviewer, about his lifelong passion for the theatre. A fascinating and entertaining insight into Dublin theatre over the course of thirty years provided by Devitt's vivid reminiscences and astute observations.

ISBN: 978-1-904505-33-4 (2008) €10

Irish Literature: Feminist Perspectives

Eds. Patricia Coughlan and Tina O'Toole

The collection discusses texts from the early 18th century to the present. A central theme of the book is the need to renegotiate the relations of feminism with nationalism and to transact the potential contest of these two important narratives, each possessing powerful emancipatory force. Irish Literature: Feminist Perspectives contributes incisively to contemporary debates about Irish culture, gender and ideology.

ISBN: 978-1-904505-35-8 (2008) €25

Silenced Voices: Hungarian Plays from Transylvania

Selected and translated by Csilla Bertha and Donald E. Morse

The five plays are wonderfully theatrical, moving fluidly from absurdism to tragedy, and from satire to the darkly comic. Donald Morse and Csilla Bertha's translations capture these qualities perfectly, giving voice to the 'forgotten playwrights of Central Europe'. They also deeply enrich our understanding of the relationship between art, ethics, and politics in Europe.

ISBN: 978-1-904505-34-1 (2008) €25

A Hazardous Melody of Being:
Seóirse Bodley's Song Cycles on the poems of Micheal O'Siadhail

Ed. Lorraine Byrne Bodley

This apograph is the first publication of Bodley's O'Siadhail song cycles and is the first book to explore the composer's lyrical modernity from a number of perspectives. Lorraine Byrne Bodley's insightful introduction describes in detail the development and essence of Bodley's musical thinking, the European influences he absorbed which linger in these cycles, and the importance of his work as a composer of the Irish art song.

ISBN: 978-1-904505-31-0 (2008) €25

Irish Theatre in England: Irish Theatrical Diaspora Series: 2

Eds. Richard Cave and Ben Levitas

Irish theatre in England has frequently illustrated the complex relations between two distinct cultures. How English reviewers and audiences interpret Irish plays is often decidedly different from how the plays were read in performance in Ireland. How certain Irish performers have chosen to be understood in Dublin is not necessarily how audiences in London have perceived their constructed stage personae. Though a collection by diverse authors, the twelve essays in this volume investigate these issues from a variety of perspectives that together chart the trajectory of Irish performance in England from the mid-nineteenth century till today.

ISBN: 978-1-904505-26-6 (2007)   €20

Goethe and Anna Amalia: A Forbidden Love?

By Ettore Ghibellino, Trans. Dan Farrelly

In this study Ghibellino sets out to show that the platonic relationship between Goethe and Charlotte von Stein – lady-in-waiting to Anna Amalia, the Dowager Duchess of Weimar – was used as part of a cover-up for Goethe's intense and prolonged love relationship with the Duchess Anna Amalia herself. The book attempts to uncover a hitherto closely-kept state secret. Readers convinced by the evidence supporting Ghibellino's hypothesis will see in it one of the very great love stories in European history – to rank with that of Dante and Beatrice, and Petrarch and Laura.

ISBN: 978-1-904505-24-2   €20

Ireland on Stage: Beckett and After

Eds. Hiroko Mikami, Minako Okamuro, Naoko Yagi

The collection focuses primarily on Irish playwrights and their work, both in text and on the stage during the latter half of the twentieth century. The central figure is Samuel Beckett, but the contributors freely draw on Beckett and his work provides a springboard to discuss contemporary playwrights such as Brian Friel, Frank McGuinness, Marina Carr and Conor McPherson amongst others. Contributors include: Anthony Roche, Hiroko Mikami, Naoko Yagi, Cathy Leeney, Joseph Long, Noreem Doody, Minako Okamuro, Christopher Murray, Futoshi Sakauchi and Declan Kiberd

ISBN: 978-1-904505-23-5 (2007)   €20

'Echoes Down the Corridor': Irish Theatre - Past, Present and Future

Eds. Patrick Lonergan and Riana O'Dwyer

This collection of fourteen new essays explores Irish theatre from exciting new perspectives. How has Irish theatre been received internationally - and, as the country becomes more multicultural, how will international theatre influence the development of drama in Ireland? These and many other important questions.

ISBN: 978-1-904505-25-9 (2007) €20

Musics of Belonging: The Poetry of Micheal O'Siadhail

Eds. Marc Caball & David F. Ford

An overall account is given of O'Siadhail's life, his work and the reception of his poetry so far. There are close readings of some poems, analyses of his artistry in matching diverse content with both classical and innovative forms, and studies of recurrent themes such as love, death, language, music, and the shifts of modern life.

ISBN: 978-1-904505-22-8 (2007) €25 (Paperback)
ISBN: 978-1-904505-21-1 (2007) €50 (Casebound)

Brian Friel's Dramatic Artistry: 'The Work has Value'

Eds. Donald E. Morse, Csilla Bertha and Maria Kurdi

Brian Friel's Dramatic Artistry presents a refreshingly broad range of voices: new work from some of the leading English-speaking authorities on Friel, and fascinating essays from scholars in Germany, Italy, Portugal, and Hungary. This book will deepen our knowledge and enjoyment of Friel's work.

ISBN: 978-1-904505-17-4 (2006) €30

The Theatre of Martin McDonagh: 'A World of Savage Stories'

Eds. Lilian Chambers and Eamonn Jordan

The book is a vital response to the many challenges set by McDonagh for those involved in the production and reception of his work. Critics and commentators from around the world offer a diverse range of often provocative approaches. What is not surprising is the focus and commitment of the engagement, given the controversial and stimulating nature of the work.

ISBN: 978-1-904505-19-8 (2006) €35

Edna O'Brien: New Critical Perspectives

Eds. Kathryn Laing, Sinead Mooney and Maureen O'Connor

The essays collected here illustrate some of the range, complexity, and interest of Edna O'Brien as a fiction writer and dramatist. They will contribute to a broader appreciation of her work and to an evolution of new critical approaches, as well as igniting more interest in the many unexplored areas of her considerable oeuvre.

ISBN: 978-1-904505-20-4 (2006) €20

Irish Theatre on Tour

Eds. Nicholas Grene and Chris Morash

'Touring has been at the strategic heart of Druid's artistic policy since the early eighties. Everyone has the right to see professional theatre in their own communities. Irish theatre on tour is a crucial part of Irish theatre as a whole'. Garry Hynes

ISBN 978-1-904505-13-6 (2005) €20

Poems 2000-2005 by Hugh Maxton

Poems 2000-2005 is a transitional collection written while the author – also known to be W.J. Mc Cormack, literary historian – was in the process of moving back from London to settle in rural Ireland.

ISBN 978-1-904505-12-9 (2005) €10

Synge: A Celebration

Ed. Colm Tóibín

A collection of essays by some of Ireland's most creative writers on the work of John Millington Synge, featuring Sebastian Barry, Marina Carr, Anthony Cronin, Roddy Doyle, Anne Enright, Hugo Hamilton, Joseph O'Connor, Mary O'Malley, Fintan O'Toole, Colm Toibin, Vincent Woods.

ISBN 978-1-904505-14-3 (2005) €15

East of Eden: New Romanian Plays

Ed. Andrei Marinescu

Four of the most promising Romanian playwrights, young and very young, are in this collection, each one with a specific way of seeing the Romanian reality, each one with a style of communicating an articulated artistic vision of the society we are living in. Ion Caramitru, General Director Romanian National Theatre Bucharest.
ISBN 978-1-904505-15-0 (2005) €10

George Fitzmaurice: 'Wild in His Own Way', Biography of an Irish Playwright

By Fiona Brennan

'Fiona Brennan's introduction to his considerable output allows us a much greater appreciation and understanding of Fitzmaurice, the one remaining under-celebrated genius of twentieth-century Irish drama'. Conall Morrison

ISBN 978-1-904505-16-7 (2005) €20

Out of History: Essays on the Writings of Sebastian Barry

Ed. Christina Hunt Mahony

The essays address Barry's engagement with the contemporary cultural debate in Ireland and also with issues that inform postcolonial critical theory. The range and selection of contributors has ensured a high level of critical expression and an insightful assessment of Barry and his works.

ISBN: 978-1-904505-18-1 (2005) €20

Three Congregational Masses

By Seoirse Bodley

'From the simpler congregational settings in the Mass of Peace and the Mass of Joy to the richer textures of the Mass of Glory, they are immediately attractive and accessible, and with a distinctively Irish melodic quality.' Barra Boydell

ISBN: 978-1-904505-11-2 (2005) €15

Georg Büchner's Woyzeck,

A new translation by Dan Farrelly

The most up-to-date German scholarship of Thomas Michael Mayer and Burghard Dedner has finally made it possible to establish an authentic sequence of scenes. The wide-spread view that this play is a prime example of loose, open theatre is no longer sustainable. Directors and teachers are challenged to "read it again".

ISBN: 978-1-904505-02-0 (2004) €10

Playboys of the Western World: Production Histories

Ed. Adrian Frazier

'The book is remarkably well-focused: half is a series of production histories of Playboy performances through the twentieth century in the UK, Northern Ireland, the USA, and Ireland. The remainder focuses on one contemporary performance, that of Druid Theatre, as directed by Garry Hynes. The various contemporary social issues that are addressed in relation to Synge's play and this performance of it give the volume an additional interest: it shows how the arts matter.' Kevin Barry

ISBN: 978-1-904505-06-8 (2004) €20

The Power of Laughter: Comedy and Contemporary Irish Theatre

Ed. Eric Weitz

The collection draws on a wide range of perspectives and voices including critics, playwrights, directors and performers. The result is a series of fascinating and provocative debates about the myriad functions of comedy in contemporary Irish theatre. Anna McMullan

As Stan Laurel said, 'it takes only an onion to cry. Peel it and weep. Comedy is harder'. 'These essays listen to the power of laughter. They hear the tough heart of Irish theatre – hard and wicked and funny'. Frank McGuinness

ISBN: 978-1-904505-05-1 (2004) €20

Sacred Play: Soul-Journeys in contemporary Irish Theatre

by Anne F. O'Reilly

'Theatre as a space or container for sacred play allows audiences to glimpse mystery and to experience transformation. This book charts how Irish playwrights negotiate the labyrinth of the Irish soul and shows how their plays contribute to a poetics of Irish culture that enables a new imagining. Playwrights discussed are: McGuinness, Murphy, Friel, Le Marquand Hartigan, Burke Brogan, Harding, Meehan, Carr, Parker, Devlin, and Barry.'

ISBN: 978-1-904505-07-5 (2004) €25

The Irish Harp Book

by Sheila Larchet Cuthbert

This is a facsimile of the edition originally published by Mercier Press in 1993. There is a new preface by Sheila Larchet Cuthbert, and the biographical material has been updated. It is a collection of studies and exercises for the use of teachers and pupils of the Irish harp.
ISBN: 978-1-904505-08-2 (2004) €35

The Drunkard

By Tom Murphy

'The Drunkard is a wonderfully eloquent play. Murphy's ear is finely attuned to the glories and absurdities of melodramatic exclamation, and even while he is wringing out its ludicrous overstatement, he is also making it sing.' The Irish Times

ISBN: 978-1-90 05-09-9 (2004) €10

Goethe: Musical Poet, Musical Catalyst

Ed. Lorraine Byrne

'Goethe was interested in, and acutely aware of, the place of music in human experience generally - and of its particular role in modern culture. Moreover, his own literary work - especially the poetry and Faust - inspired some of the major composers of the European tradition to produce some of their finest works.' Martin Swales

ISBN: 978-1-9045-10-5 (2004) €40

The Theatre of Marina Carr: "Before rules was made"

Eds. Anna McMullan & Cathy Leeney

As the first published collection of articles on the theatre of Marina Carr, this volume explores the world of Carr's theatrical imagination, the place of her plays in contemporary theatre in Ireland and abroad and the significance of her highly individual voice.

ISBN: 978-0-9534257-7-8 (2003) €20

Critical Moments: Fintan O'Toole on Modern Irish Theatre

Eds. Julia Furay & Redmond O'Hanlon

This new book on the work of Fintan O'Toole, the internationally acclaimed theatre critic and cultural commentator, offers percussive analyses and assessments of the major plays and playwrights in the canon of modern Irish theatre. Fearless and provocative in his judgements, O'Toole is essential reading for anyone interested in criticism or in the current state of Irish theatre.

ISBN: 978-1-904505-03-7 (2003) €20

Goethe and Schubert: Across the Divide

Eds. Lorraine Byrne & Dan Farrelly

Proceedings of the International Conference, 'Goethe and Schubert in Perspective and Performance', Trinity College Dublin, 2003. This volume includes essays by leading scholars – Barkhoff, Boyle, Byrne, Canisius, Dürr, Fischer, Hill, Kramer, Lamport, Lund, Meikle, Newbould, Norman McKay, White, Whitton, Wright, Youens – on Goethe's musicality and his relationship to Schubert; Schubert's contribution to sacred music and the Lied and his setting of Goethe's Singspiel, Claudine. A companion volume of this Singspiel (with piano reduction and English translation) is also available.

ISBN: 978-1-904505-04-4 (2003)   €25

Goethe's Singspiel, 'Claudine von Villa Bella'

Set by Franz Schubert

Goethe's Singspiel in three acts was set to music by Schubert in 1815. Only Act One of Schuberts's Claudine score is extant. The present volume makes Act One available for performance in English and German. It comprises both a piano reduction by Lorraine Byrne of the original Schubert orchestral score and a bilingual text translated for the modern stage by Dan Farrelly. This is a tale, wittily told, of lovers and vagabonds, romance, reconciliation, and resolution of family conflict.

ISBN: 978-0-9544290-0-3 (2002)   €20

Theatre of Sound, Radio and the Dramatic Imagination

By Dermot Rattigan

An innovative study of the challenges that radio drama poses to the creative imagination of the writer, the production team, and the listener.
"A remarkably fine study of radio drama – everywhere informed by the writer's professional experience of such drama in the making…A new theoretical and analytical approach – informative, illuminating and at all times readable." Richard Allen Cave

ISBN: 978- 0-9534-257-5-4 (2002)   €20

Talking about Tom Murphy

Ed. Nicholas Grene

Talking About Tom Murphy is shaped around the six plays in the landmark Abbey Theatre Murphy Season of 2001, assembling some of the best-known commentators on his work: Fintan O'Toole, Chris Morash, Lionel Pilkington, Alexandra Poulain, Shaun Richards, Nicholas Grene and Declan Kiberd.

ISBN: 978-0-9534-257-9-2 (2002)   €15

Hamlet: The Shakespearean Director

by Mike Wilcock

"This study of the Shakespearean director as viewed through various interpretations of HAMLET is a welcome addition to our understanding of how essential it is for a director to have a clear vision of a great play. It is an important study from which all of us who love Shakespeare and who understand the importance of continuing contemporary exploration may gain new insights." From the Foreword, by Joe Dowling, Artistic Director, The Guthrie Theater, Minneapolis, MN

ISBN: 978-1-904505-00-6 (2002) €20

The Theatre of Frank Mc Guinness: Stages of Mutability

Ed. Helen Lojek

The first edited collection of essays about internationally renowned Irish playwright Frank McGuinness focuses on both performance and text. Interpreters come to diverse conclusions, creating a vigorous dialogue that enriches understanding and reflects a strong consensus about the value of McGuinness's complex work.

ISBN: 978-1904505-01-3. (2002) €20

Theatre Talk: Voices of Irish Theatre Practitioners

Eds Lilian Chambers, Ger Fitzgibbon and Eamonn Jordan

"This book is the right approach - asking practitioners what they feel." Sebastian Barry, Playwright "... an invaluable and informative collection of interviews with those who make and shape the landscape of Irish Theatre." Ben Barnes, Artistic Director of the Abbey Theatre

ISBN: 978-0-9534-257-6-1 (2001) €20

In Search of the South African Iphigenie

By Erika von Wietersheim and Dan Farrelly

Discussions of Goethe's "Iphigenie auf Tauris" (Under the Curse) as relevant to women's issues in modern South Africa: women in family and public life; the force of women's spirituality; experience of personal relationships; attitudes to parents and ancestors; involvement with religion.

ISBN: 978-0-9534257-8-5 (2001) €10

'The Starving' and 'October Song':

Two contemporary Irish plays by Andrew Hinds

The Starving, set during and after the siege of Derry in 1689, is a moving and engrossing drama of the emotional journey of two men.

October Song, a superbly written family drama set in real time in pre-ceasefire Derry.

ISBN: 978-0-9534-257-4-7 (2001) €10

Seen and Heard: Six new plays by Irish women

Ed. Cathy Leeney

A rich and funny, moving and theatrically exciting collection of plays by Mary Elizabeth Burke-Kennedy, Síofra Campbell, Emma Donoghue, Anne Le Marquand Hartigan, Michelle Read and Dolores Walshe.

ISBN: 978-0-9534-257-3-0 (2001) €20

Theatre Stuff: Critical essays on contemporary Irish theatre

Ed. Eamonn Jordan

Best selling essays on the successes and debates of contemporary Irish theatre at home and abroad. Contributors include: Thomas Kilroy, Declan Hughes, Anna McMullan, Declan Kiberd, Deirdre Mulrooney, Fintan O'Toole, Christopher Murray, Caoimhe McAvinchey and Terry Eagleton.

ISBN: 978-0-9534-2571-1-6 (2000) €20

Under the Curse. Goethe's "Iphigenie Auf Tauris", A New Version

By Dan Farrelly

The Greek myth of Iphigenie grappling with the curse on the house of Atreus is brought vividly to life. This version is currently being used in Johannesburg to explore problems of ancestry, religion, and Black African women's spirituality.

ISBN: 978-09534-257-8-5 (2000) €10

Urfaust, A New Version of Goethe's early "Faust" in Brechtian Mode

By Dan Farrelly

This version is based on Brecht's irreverent and daring re-interpretation of the German classic. "Urfaust is a kind of well-spring for German theatre… The love-story is the most daring and the most profound in German dramatic literature." Brecht

ISBN: 978-0-9534-257-0-9 (1998)   €20